STUDY GUIDE SERIES

THE NEW TESTAMENT

MARK

Freshly translated by Nicholas King

For Michael and Frances-Anne, with love

First published in 2006 by
KEVIN MAYHEW LTD
Buxhall, Stowmarket, Suffolk, IP14 3BW
E-mail: info@kevinmayhewltd.com
www.kevinmayhew.com

Mark first appeared in Nicholas King's translation of *The New Testament*.

9 8 7 6 5 4 3 2 1 0

ISBN 1 84417 528 6
Catalogue No. 1500886

Cover Design: Jonathan Stroulger
Editors: Peter Dainty, Marian Reid
Typesetting: Richard Weaver

Set in Simoncini Garamond and *Abadi MT Lt It*

Nihil Obstat: This translation has been examined by the Theology Committee of the Bishops' Conference of England and Wales and is declared free from doctrinal error. It is not authorised for use in the Liturgy of the Church and is approved for publication, in accord with Canon 825§1.

Mgr Andrew Summersgill, General Secretary, 8 June 2004

Printed and bound in Great Britain

Introduction

Kevin Mayhew's invitation to prepare Mark's Gospel for publication as a separate volume has made me go back to that Gospel with a fresh eye; and I am glad of it, for it has renewed my immense fondness for the Gospel that is printed second in our New Testaments. One must never have favourites, of course, but there are certainly days of the week when I think that if I were to have one, then Mark would be it.

Mark is the shortest of the Gospels, and in the view of most scholars the earliest, so that it was very likely he who invented the genre. Its brevity should not put you off, however. St Augustine, who thought that Mark wrote after Matthew, was a bit dismissive of our evangelist, regarding him as no better than an abbreviator or summariser.

Mark wrote his Gospel, I think, to answer two questions: First, who is Jesus? Second, given that Jesus is so, what must his disciples be like? Mark's answer to these two great questions is not put before us 'on a plate'; we are made to struggle for it, through the mysterious parables of chapter 4, and through a series of haunting ambiguities and unanswered questions. Look out for these questions as you go through, and consider what answer the evangelist wants us to give to the following:

'Who can forgive sin, except one person, namely God?' (2:7)

'Who is this then? Because both the wind and the sea obey him.' (4:41)

and (on Jesus' lips) 'Why do you call me good?
No one is good, except one, God.' (10:18)

Or look closely at the account of Jesus' death, and ask what possible evidence the centurion can have for saying 'Truly this man was Son of God' (15:39), and ask yourself why Mark puts this verdict at just this point, making it the climax of his exposition of the mystery of Jesus. And why did he end his Gospel with that extraordinary sentence 'And they said nothing to anybody. For they were afraid', sketching an enigmatic question mark in the air?

And as for the disciples, see how often they open their mouths only to put their foot in it, as the saying goes. Is there anything they can actually get right? The women, by contrast, with the exception of Herod's wife and daughter, are always models of what disciples should be.

Mark is also a gifted writer. His Greek is, one cannot deny it, rather rough in places (I have tried to preserve his ruggedness and vigour in the translation), and Matthew often purses his lips and tidies it up, in schoolmasterly fashion; but it is powerful, and Mark can manage several different moods. Contrast, for example, the breathless pace and energy of the first two chapters (and count the number of times he uses the word 'immediately', to keep the narrative moving), with the slow and sombre build-up to the Passion, as the darkness deepens from chapter 8 onwards. Mark has great skill in his use of language, to achieve just the right effect, and I hope that you will savour and admire it, and hear the voice of the One who said, up there on the mountain, 'This is my Son, the beloved. Listen to him' (9:7).

According to Mark

The Title

1 [1] Beginning of the good news of Jesus Messiah Son of God.

With this characteristically curt announcement we start our reading of the first of the Gospels to be written. 'Beginning' tells the reader where we are, of course, but may also serve as an echo of the opening words of the Bible. 'Good news' (in Greek, euangelion*) has come, through the Anglo-Saxon 'god-spel', into English as 'gospel'. It reflects on the one hand an Old Testament background, where the word refers to the proclamation of God's great deeds, and on the other hand a background in the Roman Empire, where it can be used for something like the announcement of a birth to the royal house, or a Roman victory in far-off places. 'Messiah' comes into Greek as 'Christ', but in this Gospel, as opposed to the letters of Paul, it is a title rather than a name. 'Son of God' is not in all manuscripts, but it is likely to be what Mark wrote, and is almost certainly what he meant.*

The emergence of John the Baptist

2-6 As it is written in Isaiah the Prophet:

'Look! I am sending my messenger before your face,
who will prepare your way;
a voice of one shouting in the desert:
"Prepare the way of the Lord,
make straight his paths."'

There arose John, baptising in the desert and proclaiming a baptism of repentance for forgiveness of sins. And there journeyed out to him the whole Judaean region, and all the Jerusalemites, and they wanted to get baptised by him in the River Jordan, confessing their sins.

And John was clothed in camel-hair; and there was a leather belt about his loins. And he was eating locusts and wild honey.

Mark's is a mysterious Gospel, and it is mysterious from the very beginning. The quotation that he attributes to Isaiah is not in fact wholly from that source. The opening lines of it are from either Exodus 23:20 (in the Greek version) or from Malachi 3:1. Only after that does Mark revert to Isaiah (40:3, in the Greek version). Why is this so? The reader must decide – but you can exclude any idea that Mark didn't know his Old Testament.

Also mysterious is the fact that Mark starts his Gospel, not with Jesus (as you might expect), but with John the Baptist. This must mean that in some sense John gives a clue to the mystery – including, apparently, that Jesus may properly be called 'Lord' in a passage that clearly referred originally to God.

We notice that John's mission (and therefore presumably that of Jesus) has something to do with confronting the reality of sin ('a baptism of repentance for the forgiveness of sins . . . confessing their sins'). We also note, with perhaps a slight shudder, John's austere clothing and unattractive diet.

How does John make you feel?

The message of John the Baptist

7, 8 And he started proclaiming, saying: 'The Stronger-One-Than-Me is coming after me, of whom I am not worthy to stoop down and untie the thong of his sandals. I baptised you with water, while he will baptise you by the Holy Spirit.'

John's message turns out to be all about Jesus, pointing to Jesus' superiority: Jesus is 'stronger', incomparably superior (the task of untying sandals was a slave's job), and his baptism is 'with the Holy Spirit', a notion that Mark has yet to explain to us.

The baptism of Jesus

9-11 And it happened in those days Jesus came from Nazareth of Galilee and was baptised into the Jordan by John. And immediately coming up out of the water he saw the heavens dividing and the Spirit like a dove coming down upon him. And a voice came out of the heavens:

'You are my Son, the beloved; in you I have taken pleasure.'

We may puzzle at this, as perhaps the early Christians did: if Jesus is so superior to John, why did he have to be baptised by him? Mark does not really give us an answer, except that a) Jesus sees the heavens dividing (which means that what happens is God's doing), and the Holy Spirit descending (as John the Baptist had indicated) and b) Jesus is publicly affirmed as God's Son. We watch with renewed interest.

What does it mean to call Jesus God's Beloved Son?

Jesus in the desert

12, 13 And immediately the Spirit hurls him out into the desert. And he was in the desert forty days being tested by the Satan, and he was with the beasts. And the angels began to serve him.

There is a breathless, urgent quality in these early chapters, partly engendered by Mark's repetition of the word 'immediately' (How many times does he use this word in the first two chapters?). What the Spirit does here is normally translated as 'sent', but the word is more powerful than this might suggest. And notice the 'historic present' ('he hurls' for 'he hurled'), which Mark favours; I have left it so in the translation, to give the 'feel' of the original.

The beginning of Jesus' mission

14, 15 Now after John had been handed over, Jesus came to Galilee proclaiming the good news of God and saying, 'The right-time has been fulfilled and the kingdom of God has drawn near. Repent and believe in the good news.'

Note the starkness of this: the moment when the mission begins is the moment of the arrest of the 'Forerunner'. There is great urgency in Jesus' proclamation: it is **now** *that a decision is required. Like John, Jesus tells his hearers that they must repent, but he also tells them to 'believe the good news'. This is the second time the term 'good news' has been used in the Gospel. What do you think it means?*

The sudden calling of two sets of brothers

16-20 And going along by the Sea of Galilee he saw Simon and Andrew the brother of Simon casting in the sea (for they were fishermen). And Jesus said to them, 'Come here, after me, and I'll make you become fishers of human beings.' And immediately abandoning their nets they followed him.

And going a little further he saw James the son of Zebedee and John his brother – and them in the boat repairing their nets. And immediately he called them. And abandoning their father Zebedee in the boat with the hirelings they went off after him.

Notice that this episode takes place 'by the Sea of Galilee'. You will see that whenever we hear this phrase in Mark, something important is about to happen. The call is a very striking one: first Simon, and his brother with the Greek name, simply leave everything to follow Jesus, without complaint or excuse, or even any apparent surprise, perhaps in response to the little joke about becoming 'fishers of human beings'. Then two other brothers answer the call, with the added detail that they abandon their father Zebedee and his staff.

Mark's Gospel is written to answer two questions: 'Who is Jesus?', and 'What must Jesus' disciples be like?' Does this episode help to answer these questions?

In the synagogue at Caphernaum

21-28 And they enter into Caphernaum. And immediately on the Sabbath going into the synagogue he began to teach. And they were amazed at his teaching. For he was teaching them as though he had authority, and not like the scribes.

And immediately there was in their synagogue a man with an unclean spirit and he shouted out, saying, 'What do we have to do with you, Jesus Nazarene? You have come to destroy us. I know who you are, the Holy One of God.' And Jesus scolded him, saying, 'Shut up and come out of him.'And the unclean spirit, convulsing and crying with a great cry, came out of him. And they were all astonished, so that they debated with each other, saying, 'What's this? New teaching with authority? He even gives instructions to the unclean spirits, and they obey him.'

And his reputation immediately went out into the whole surrounding area of the Galilee.

Now we see Jesus, for the first time in the Gospel, doing something that is an important part of Mark's understanding of him, namely teaching. The teaching has an immediate effect: 'they were amazed'. We shall see this 'amazement' again and again in the Gospel, describing Jesus' impact on people, especially disciples. His teaching is also 'with authority', we gather. 'Authority' is another word to look out for throughout the Gospel. We also see the first mention of 'the scribes', who are going to represent (largely but not wholly – see 12:28-34) Jesus' opponents. Here already we can detect the tension.

Jesus displays effortless 'authority', telling unclean spirits where they get off, even though they try to exercise power over him by correctly identifying him as 'Jesus Nazarene – the Holy One of God'. They can do nothing against him, however.

Notice that Jesus is said to 'scold' the unclean spirit. There will be other uses of this verb in the course of the Gospel. Who else is scolded, and who does the scolding?

'What's this?' say the crowds. What is ***your*** *answer?*

Simon Peter's mother-in-law

29-31 And immediately coming out of the synagogue they came into the house of Simon and of Andrew with James and John. Now the mother-in-law of Simon lay sick, fevered. And immediately they tell him about her. And approaching he raised her up, taking her hand. And the fever abandoned her. And she was serving them.

This healing is, as always with Jesus' miracles, effortless. It shows, moreover, Jesus' complete indifference to questions of ritual purity: he touches someone who is a woman, and perhaps on the point of death. Finally, the healing brings her to a point where she can do 'service', the proud task of angels (1:13) and of Jesus himself (10:45) and of Jesus' disciples.

Does this episode take us deeper into the mysterious question of who Jesus is and what his disciples must be like?

Healings, once the Sabbath is over

32-34 When it grew late, when the sun set, they brought to him all those who were in a bad way, including those who had demons. And the entire city was gathered at the door. And he cured many who were in a bad way with various diseases. And he hurled out many demons and he did not allow the demons to speak because they knew him.

Here Mark gives us a little picture of what it was all like: Jesus' reputation has spread, and once the Sabbath is over people can bring their sick to him. His impact is immense: 'The entire city was gathered at the door.'

Notice the command to silence (sometimes called the 'Messianic Secret'). This is the first of many times that we shall meet it. Here it is addressed to the demons, 'because they knew him'. Why do you think that Jesus insists on secrecy? (Later on, we shall see that, as you might expect, no one takes any notice of the command.)

Jesus at prayer; Jesus misunderstood; Jesus continues the mission

35-38 And early in the morning, when it was deep in the night, rising up he went out and went away to a deserted place. And there he began to pray. And Simon and those with him went chasing after him. And they tell him, 'Everyone is looking for you.' And he says to them, 'Let's go elsewhere, to the neighbouring market towns, so that I may proclaim there also. Because for this I came out.'

We go further into the mystery of who Jesus is. Here we note that he is one who needs to pray. We note also that 'Simon' (already taking on a certain prominence in the group) really does not understand him and clearly regards this prayer business as a waste of time. We should, however, be startled, on reading the story, to notice that Jesus neither scolds Simon for interrupting his prayer-life, nor grudgingly consents to come back with them; instead he takes us by surprise and points out new directions for his mission. Is this the effect of prayer?

Teaching, proclamation, exorcism, the healing of a leper

39-45 And he went into their synagogues, into the whole of the Galilee, proclaiming, and hurling out demons. And a leper comes to him, begging him, falling on his knees and telling him, 'If you want, you can make me clean.' And taking pity, stretching out his hand, he touched him and tells him, 'I do want: be made clean'. And immediately the leprosy went away from him, and he was made clean. And sternly warning him he immediately drove him out. And he tells him, 'See that you say nothing to anybody. Instead, go, show yourself, and make the offering that Moses prescribed with regard to your cleansing, as a witness to them.' But he went out and he started to proclaim many things and to spread the word; so that he could no longer go into a city; instead, he was outside, in deserted places. And they started to come to him from all sides.

This first chapter leaves us quite out of breath as it comes to its end, if we have been trying to keep up with Jesus, as we watch him travelling, teaching, 'hurling out demons'. Then there comes a major test, the encounter with the highly contagious disease of leprosy. We repress a shudder as Jesus actually touches the leper; then he states his determination to 'make him clean', and the leprosy disappears as easily as Simon's mother-in-law's fever. Once again there is the command to silence.

Notice the uncertainty about the identity of 'he', 'him', 'them' in this passage. It is a difficulty in reading Mark that we often have to guess whom his pronouns are referring to.

What do you make of Jesus so far?

The paralytic who came through the roof

2 1-12 And coming again into Caphernaum several days later, it was heard that he was in [the] house. And many gathered so that he could no longer go, not even to the door, and he began to speak to them The Message. And they came, carrying to him a paralytic lifted up by four [people]. And not being able to bring [him] to him, because of the crowd, they unroofed the roof [of the house] where he was, and digging out [the clay of the roof?] they let down the mattress where the paralytic lay. And seeing their faith Jesus says to the paralytic, 'Child, your sins are forgiven.' Now there were some of the scribes sitting, and arguing in their hearts, 'Why does this fellow speak in this way? He blasphemes. Who can forgive sin, except one person, namely God?' And immediately Jesus, knowing in his spirit that they were arguing in their hearts in this way, says to them, 'Why do you argue these things in your heart? What is easier, to say to the paralytic, "Your sins are forgiven you," or to say "Arise and take up your mattress and walk"? But so that you may know that the Son of Man has authority to forgive sins on earth' – he says to the paralytic – 'To you I say, arise, take up your mattress, and go to your house.' And he arose and immediately taking up the mattress he went out before all of them.

The result was that all were beside themselves, and glorified God, saying, 'Like this we never saw.'

We are supposed to be startled by a number of things here. There is the breathless sense of the crowds surrounding Jesus, dramatically signalled by the unusual rearrangement of the roof. There is the unreferred 'he' (who can only be Jesus) in the first line. There is the reference to the 'house' (possibly that of Simon and Andrew, the only one we have previously seen). The 'house' in Mark's Gospel is often (though not here) a place where Jesus gives private instruction to his disciples.

The next thing to startle us is what Jesus says: not, as we may have been expecting, some command to the paralysis to depart, but, to the paralytic, 'Child, your sins are forgiven.' This assertion of the man's status as child may perhaps be related to Jesus' sense of God as 'Father'. This has only been hinted at so far in the Gospel, with the two references to Jesus as 'Son'. And the forgiveness of sins, presumably a diagnosis of what was **really** *wrong with the man, is a great shock. And it is not only the reader who is shocked. Rather surprisingly, we learn that 'some of the scribes' (who have already been dismissed as being less impressive teachers than Jesus) were 'sitting there', and take this quite amiss. They immediately raise the question whether Jesus is claiming a function reserved to God. Jesus doesn't trouble to answer them, but offers them the expected healing as a proof that 'the Son of Man has authority (that word again) to forgive sins on earth'.*

Who is this Son of Man? Clearly Jesus; but it is the first time we have met the expression, which reads like a title of some sort. We shall watch carefully for it in future. Some scholars prefer to translate it as something like 'the Human One', to preserve inclusive language; but a) it clearly refers only to Jesus, and b) it was clearly an expression that was frequently on Jesus' lips, so I have judged it worth the risk of leaving it as it stands.

Two other things: 'The Message' is capitalised because Mark has put it in a curiously emphatic place in the sentence. And, second, the result of the episode is to direct praise, not to Jesus, but first to God: 'the result was that all were beside themselves, and glorified God'.

Jesus and revenue collectors

13-17 And he went out again, beside the sea. And the whole crowd came to him, and he was teaching them. And passing by he saw Levi of Alphaeus sitting at the revenue office. And he says to him, 'Follow me.' And rising up he followed him.

And it happens that he is lying down [to dine] in his house, and many revenue collectors and sinners lay down [to dine] with Jesus and with his disciples. For they were many, and they followed him.

And the scribes of the Pharisees, seeing that he was eating with sinners and revenue collectors, started saying to his disciples, 'He's eating with revenue collectors and sinners.' Jesus overheard and says to them, 'The strong do not have need of a doctor, but those who are in a bad way. I did not come to call the just, but sinners.'

Once again, this important episode takes place 'beside the sea'; once more, Jesus attracts the crowds. There is a new departure here, however, in that Jesus is seen in company with some far-from-desirable friends, the associates of the 'revenue collector', Levi of Alphaeus. The main thing to notice, though, is how instantly Levi responds to the command: 'follow me'. This leads to a celebration with some equally undesirable characters, which raises some more disapproving questions from the 'scribes' (this time the 'scribes of the Pharisees'). Jesus then announces his rather subversive mission-statement: 'I did not come to call the just, but sinners.'

Might people be shocked at Jesus regarding **you** *as a friend?*

Jesus' disciples don't fast!

18-22 And the disciples of John, and the Pharisees, were fasting. And they come and say to him, 'Why do the disciples of John, and the disciples of the Pharisees fast, but your disciples do not fast?' And Jesus said to them, 'Surely the sons of the bridal chamber can't fast during the time when the bridegroom is with them? As long as they have the bridegroom with them, they cannot fast. But days will come when the bridegroom is taken away from them, and then they will fast on that day.

'No one sows a patch of new cloth on an old garment. Otherwise, the new one takes the fullness away from the old one, and the tear becomes worse.

'And no one pours new wine into old wineskins. Otherwise the wine will break the skins, and so both the wine and the skins are destroyed. So: New Wine into New Flasks.'

Clearly Jesus has been identified as a figure of religious significance; so, his opponents (now Pharisees and followers of the Baptist) ask aggressively, why don't his disciples behave more religiously? The answer that Jesus' critics are given is in terms of a wedding: he is the bridegroom in God's wedding-feast, and now is the moment for celebration, not fasting. Jesus tells his first two 'parables' to support his point, about patching old garments, and about bottling new wine. Either way, the message is the same: Jesus is Different.

Is Jesus different?

Jesus' disciples don't keep Sabbath

23-28 And it happened that on the Sabbath he was journeying through the sown fields, and his disciples started to make their way plucking the ears of corn. And the Pharisees said to him, 'Look: they are doing something on the Sabbath for which there is no authority.' And he says to them, 'Did you never read what David did, when he had need, and he and those with him were hungry, how he entered the house of God, in the days of Abiathar the priest, and devoured the loaves of presentation, which no one except the priests has authority to eat, and he gave them to those who were with him?' And he said to them, 'The Sabbath came into existence for the sake of human beings, and not human beings for the sake of the Sabbath, so that the Son of Man is Lord also of the Sabbath.'

Once again, Jesus' disciples cause trouble, this time by performing an activity that is forbidden on the Sabbath, which seems odd, given that they are followers of a clearly religious figure. Jesus defends his followers with an adroit reference to 1 Samuel 21:1-7, which reveals him as an attentive and imaginative student of Scripture. But there is a deeper point to be made here: who is the Sabbath for? And underlying all this is Jesus' implicit claim to have authority over the Sabbath. That is a high claim indeed.

Notice that Jesus is not questioning Sabbath observance, so much as the Pharisees' interpretations of it.

Healing on the Sabbath (in a synagogue!) – and a plot to commit murder

3 1-6 And he came back into the synagogue; and there was there a man who had his hand dried up. And they watched him, in case he should heal him on the Sabbath, so that they could accuse him. And he says to the man who had the dried hand, 'Rise up into the middle.' And he says to them, 'Is there authority on the Sabbath to do good or to do evil? To save a life or to kill?' But they were silent. And looking around them with anger, grieving with [at] the hardness of their heart, he says to the man, 'Stretch out your hand.' And he stretched it out. And his hand was restored.

And the Pharisees, going out immediately, hatched a conspiracy with the Herodians against him, how they might destroy him.

We go deeper into the mystery of who Jesus is: and we notice that the opposition is now overt ('they watched him'), and that by the end of the story it is turning to killing, as the unlikely combination of the 'Herodians' and the Pharisees conspires to put an end to it all. Jesus' response is purely religious, while their response is clearly wrong, from the very beginning.

Why do you think Jesus arouses so much opposition?

A summary of Jesus' activities

7-12 And Jesus with his disciples went up to the Sea. And a great number from the Galilee followed [him]. And from Judaea, and from Jerusalem and from Idumaea and across the Jordan and around Tyre and Sidon, a great number, hearing what things he was doing, came to him. And he told his disciples that a boat should be ready for him, on account of the crowd, so that they should not press upon him. For he cured many, so that whoever had afflictions fell upon him, that they might touch him.

And the unclean spirits, whenever they saw him, fell down before him, and cried out, saying, 'You are the Son of God.' And often he scolded them, that they should not make him known.

Once again we meet the 'Sea of Galilee'; here it functions as the setting for crowds, and healings, and exorcisms, and commands to secrecy about Jesus' status as 'Son of God'.

Appointment of the Twelve

13-19 And he goes up to the mountain, and he summons whom he wanted. And they came to him. And he made twelve, that they should be with him, and that he should send them to proclaim, and to have authority to throw out the demons. And he made twelve. And he put the name on Simon of 'Rock'. And James the [son] of Zebedee and John the brother of James, and he put the name on them of Boanerges, which is 'sons of thunder'. And Andrew and Philip and Bartholomew and Matthew and Thomas and James of Alphaeus and Thaddaeus and Simon the Canaanite. And Judas Iscariot, who also betrayed him.

The selection of his 'core group' now takes place. Presumably the fact that there are twelve of them represents Jesus' intention of founding a 'new Israel'. We notice Jesus' tendency to give nicknames: 'Rock', 'Boanerges', and perhaps 'the Canaanite' and 'Iscariot', though this is less certain. Two of the disciples (Andrew and Philip) have Greek rather than Hebrew or Aramaic names, which is striking, especially since Andrew's brother Simon has a perfectly respectable Hebrew or Aramaic name. We note the final phrase, 'who also betrayed him', and reflect, perhaps, that this is true of all of them. We may also observe the three functions of disciples: to be with him, to proclaim, and to have authority to cast out demons.

Are the 'Twelve' model disciples?

Jesus the embarrassing

20-35 And he comes to [the] house. And again the crowd comes together, so that they could not even eat bread. And 'his people' hearing [it] came out to arrest him. For they said, 'He's beside himself.' And the scribes who came down from Jerusalem said, 'He has Beelzeboul' and 'It is by the ruler of the demons that he casts out the demons.' And summoning them in parables he began to say to them, 'How can Satan cast out Satan?' And, 'If a kingdom is divided against itself, that kingdom cannot stand.' And, 'If a house is divided against itself, that house cannot stand. And so if Satan rose up against himself and is divided, he cannot stand; his end is coming. But no one can enter the house of the strong one to plunder his property unless he first binds the strong one and then plunders his house. Amen I tell you, all their sins and all their blasphemies that they blaspheme will be forgiven to human beings. But whoever blasphemes against the Holy Spirit, does not have forgiveness for ever, but is guilty of an everlasting sin.' This was because they said, 'He has an unclean spirit.'

And his mother and his brothers come; and standing outside they sent to him, calling him. And a crowd sat about him, and they tell him, 'Look: your mother and your brothers and your sisters are outside. They are looking for you.'

And answering he says to them, 'Who is my mother, and brothers?' And looking round at those who sat about him in a circle, he says, 'Look – my mother and my brothers. Whoever does the will of God, that person is my brother and sister and mother.'

Jesus now visibly embarrasses 'his people', who try to arrest him. In that culture, it was of immense importance that one should be seen to be honouring the values of the clan; and failure to do so might be evidence of insanity.

'Scribes from Jerusalem' now join 'Jesus' people', the fourth time that these characters have been mentioned. Each time it has signalled trouble. Here they make the offensive accusation that Jesus is allied to Beelzeboul, and that's how he casts out demons. Jesus exposes the shaky logic of their argument, but probably does not win any friends among them, especially when he accuses them of committing the unforgivable sin of 'blaspheming against the Holy Spirit'.

After this interlude, Jesus' family send for him, and he resists, perhaps even giving them a brush-off. We may, however, take heart from his statement that anyone who does God's will is Jesus' 'brother and sister and mother': the idea of family is redefined.

Do you belong to Jesus' family? What effect, if any, does following Jesus have on your family life?

The setting for the parables; the first parable (the Sower), and an explanation of it

4 1-20 And again he began to teach by the sea; and a very great crowd gathers to him, so that he boards a ship and sits on the sea, and the whole crowd was facing the sea, on land. And he began to teach them many things in parables, and he said to them in his teachings, 'Listen – Look! The sower went out to sow, and it happened as he sowed that some fell beside the road, and the birds came and devoured it. And other [seed] fell on the rocky ground, where there was not much earth. And immediately it sprang up, because it had no depth of earth; and when the sun rose it was scorched, and because it had no root it was dried up. And other [seed] fell on thorns, and the thorns came up and suffocated it, and it did not yield fruit. And other [seeds] fell on good earth, and yielded fruit, coming up and growing, and it bore as much as thirty times, and even sixty times, and a hundred.' And he said, 'Whoever has ears to hear, let them hear.'

And when he was alone, those with him, with the twelve, asked him [about] the parables. And he said to them, 'To you the mystery is given of the kingdom of God; whereas to those outside everything happens in parables, so that

"Looking they may look and not see
and hearing they may hear and not understand
lest they return and it be forgiven them."'

And he says to them, 'Do you not know this parable – and how will you know all the other parables? The sower is sowing the word. But these are the ones beside the road, where the word is sown; and when they hear, immediately Satan comes, and takes the word that is sown into them. And those likewise [are] the ones who are sown on the rocky bits, who whenever they hear the word immediately accept it with joy, and do not have root in themselves, but are momentary, then when there comes trouble or persecution on account of the word, they are immediately made to stumble. And others there are who are sown into the thorns: these are the ones who hear the word, and the concerns of the world, and the deceit of wealth, and desire for all the other things march in and suffocate the word, and it becomes sterile. And these are the ones who are sown into good earth, who hear the word and receive it and bear fruit, in thirties and sixties and hundreds.'

Mark has told us that Jesus is a teacher 'with authority'. Now he actually lets us hear some of the things that Jesus teaches. Our attention is carefully focused: once again we are by 'the Sea'; once again there is a huge crowd, and Jesus is forced to a striking expedient, that of sitting on a boat (Mark expresses it slightly uncomfortably, that he 'sits on the sea'; but we know what he means).

Then comes this well-known parable; and, for the first time (of many) in Mark, the disciples completely fail to understand, and Jesus has (reluctantly, we feel) to explain the parable to them.

What is the parable supposed to tell us? Are parables meant to conceal or to reveal the meaning of Jesus' teaching?

Three (or four) more parables

21-34 And he said to them, 'Surely the lamp does not come so as to be put under the bushel or under the bed? Is it not intended to be put on the lamp-stand? For there is nothing hidden, except so that it should be revealed; nor did it become obscured, except that it should come into the open. If anyone has ears to hear, let them hear.'

And he said to them, 'Look at what you hear. In the measure that you measure out it will be measured out to you, and it will be added to you. For whoever has, it will be given to that person. And whoever does not have, even what they have will be taken away from them.'

And he said, 'So is the kingdom of God, as a man sows seed on the earth; and he sleeps and wakes, night and day, and the seed sprouts and lengthens, in a way that he himself does not know. The earth yields fruit automatically, first a stalk of grain, then an ear, then full corn in the ear. But when the fruit comes, immediately "he sends out the sickle, because the harvest has drawn near".'

And he said, 'How shall we liken the kingdom of God, or in what parable shall we place it? It is like a grain of mustard, which when it is sown into the earth, being smaller than all the seeds which are on the earth. And when it is sown, it comes up and becomes bigger than all the vegetables, and it makes big branches, so that "under its shadow the birds of the air find shade".'

And with many such parables he spoke the word to them, just as they were able to hear. But apart from a parable, he did not speak to them; but privately to his own disciples he explained everything.

Mark continues to give us the flavour of Jesus' teaching, its combination of plain commonsense and obscurity; and there is a feeling that Jesus wanted his disciples to grasp it, but others to remain uninitiated.

The quotation about 'he sends out the sickle' is from Joel 4:13; that about the 'birds of the air' is from Ezekiel 17:23.

Why the parables, do you think?

Who *is* this, then?

35-41 And he says to them on that day, as it grew late, 'Let us go through to the other side.' And abandoning the crowd, they took him as he was in the boat. And other boats were with him. And there comes a great storm of wind, and the waves beat upon and into the boat; so that already the boat was beginning to be filled. And he was in the stern, sleeping on the pillow. And they arouse him and say to him, 'Teacher, don't you care that we are being destroyed?' And being thoroughly aroused, he scolded the wind, and said to the sea, 'Silence; be quiet'; and there came a great calm. And he says to them, 'Why are you such cowards? How do you not have faith?' And they feared, a great fear. And they said to each other, 'Who is this, then? Because both the wind and the sea obey him.'

This is a remarkable story; Mark is not particularly interested in geographical details, but gets Jesus and his disciples to cross the Sea of Galilee. As often happens in these parts, a storm comes up unexpectedly, and the disciples panic, accusing Jesus of indifference to their fate. Like someone calming a boisterous dog, Jesus orders the sea to behave (and it does), then rebukes the disciples, for the first time indicating the importance of faith to them. Their response (again for the first time in this Gospel) is to 'fear a great fear'; this is a reaction that in the Old Testament signals the presence of God. Then we hear the question they ask themselves: 'Who is this, then?' It is a question that Mark does not answer. Instead, he invites the reader to respond: who **is** *this, then?*

The possessed man in the land of the Gerasenes

5 1-20 And they came to the other side of the sea, into the land of the Gerasenes. And as he came out of the boat, immediately there met him out of the tombs a man with an unclean spirit, who had his dwelling among the tombs. And not even with chains could anyone bind him, on account of the fact that he had often been bound with fetters and chains. And the chains and the fetters had been torn apart by him, and broken. And no one was strong enough to tame him. And all night and day he was in the tombs and in the mountains, shouting out and cutting himself with stones. And seeing Jesus from afar he ran and worshipped him, and shouting in a loud voice he says, 'What have you to do with me, Jesus, Son of the Most High God? I conjure you by God, do not torture me.' For he was saying to him, 'Come out, unclean spirit, from the man.' And he asked him, 'What name [do they give] to you?' And he said to him, 'Legion is the name [they give] to me, because we are many.' And he begged him, many times over, not to send them out of the region. And there was there, near the mountain, a large herd of pigs feeding. And they begged him, saying, 'Send us into the pigs, that we may enter into them.' And he allowed them. And the unclean spirits going out went into the pigs, and the herd rushed down the slope into the sea, about two thousand, and they suffocated in the sea. And those who looked after them fled and announced into the city and into the fields. And they came to see what had happened. And they come to Jesus, and they see the possessed man sitting

down, clothed and sober, the one who had had the Legion. And they were afraid. And those who saw explained to them how it happened to the possessed man, and about the pigs. And they began to beg him to go away from their frontiers. And as he was going on board the boat, the man who had been possessed begged him that he might be with him. And he did not allow him, but says to him, 'Go into your house, to your people, and announce to them what things the Lord has done for you and had mercy on you.' And he went off and began to proclaim in the Decapolis what Jesus had done for him. And they were all amazed.

This is yet another extraordinary story from Mark. He emphasises what a powerful opponent Jesus has here, one who dwells 'among the tombs' (something to make Mark's readers shiver); he cannot be shackled, despite numerous attempts; he shouts, and he mutilates himself. Despite all this, he runs to Jesus, worships him, and correctly identifies him as Son of God. Jesus, without turning a hair, a) discovers the demon's name, and we whistle sharply as we discover that there may have been as many as six thousand unclean spirits, b) as a special favour allows the demons to go into the nearby pigs, but their respite is illusory, since c) they drown anyway. Not surprisingly, the news of this gets about, and instead of applauding the man's healing, the locals get nervous, and get rid of Jesus. The healed man wants to stay with him; but you can't choose discipleship – it is discipleship that chooses you, and instead the man is told to go and preach at home. The effect on his compatriots is one we have encountered before, and shall see again: 'they were all amazed'.

How many different reactions to Jesus are there in this story? Which ones are correct?

Two stories 'sandwiched' round each other

21-43 And when Jesus had crossed in the boat back to the other side, a great crowd gathered upon him. And he was by the sea. And one of the synagogue rulers comes to him, Jairus by name, and seeing him he falls at his feet and begs him many things, saying, 'My little daughter is in extremis; do come and lay hands on her, so that she may be saved and may live.' And he went with him. And a great crowd followed him and they pressed upon him.

And a woman, who had been in haemorrhage for twelve years, and had suffered many things from many doctors, and had spent all that she had, and she was no way helped, but rather she went downhill, having heard the things about Jesus, coming in the crowd from behind touched his garment. For she was saying [to herself], 'If I were just to touch his garments, I shall be saved.' And immediately the fountain of her blood was dried up, and she knew in her body that she was healed from her scourge. And immediately, Jesus, knowing in himself that the power had gone out of him, turning round in the crowd said, 'Who touched my garments?' And his disciples said to him, 'You see the crowd pressing upon you, and you say, "Who touched me?".' And he looked about to see the woman who had done this. And the woman, afraid and trembling, knowing what had happened to her, came and fell before him, and told him the whole truth. And he said to her, 'Daughter, your faith has saved you. Go in peace, and be healed of your affliction.'

While he was still speaking, they come from the [house of the] synagogue ruler, saying, 'Your daughter died. Why still bother the teacher?' But Jesus, overhearing the message being uttered, says to the synagogue ruler, 'Do not be afraid. Only believe.' And he did not allow anyone to follow along with him except Peter and James and John the brother of James. And they came to the house of the synagogue ruler and he sees a disturbance, and people weeping, and wailing loudly. And going in he says to them, 'Why do you make a tumult and weep? The child is not dead but asleep.' And they jeered at him. And he threw them all out, and takes the father of the child, and the mother, and those with him, and he goes in where the child was. And taking the hand of the child, he says to her, 'Talitha Koum', which in translation is, 'Little girl, I say to you, arise.' And immediately the little girl arose and walked. For she was twelve years old. And immediately they were beside themselves with great ecstasy. And he strongly commanded them that no one should know this. And he said that she be given [something] to eat. And he went out from there.

Mark employs a technique that we may call 'sandwiching', wrapping one story round another, so that each story sheds light on the other. Here it is the story of Jairus's daughter that is 'sandwiched' around the story of the woman with the flow of blood. The woman's story is a charming one: she is utterly alone, for her condition alienates her from all human contact, even from her family, and therefore from any sense of self-worth, and even, we may deduce, from God. She shows initiative, however, more than any disciple so far. We are even allowed to hear what she thinks: 'If I were just to touch his garments', and what she wants: 'I shall be saved'. She is **healed** *(but not yet saved), and knows it; Jesus also knows it, despite the uncomprehending jeers of his disciples, and he knows that it is a woman who has touched him. She confesses all, 'afraid and trembling', like those other women at the Gospel's end (16:8), then hears those lovely words: 'Daughter, your faith has saved you.'*

The other story likewise gives us great joy. Somewhat unexpectedly, it is a synagogue-ruler who asks Jesus for help (and we are even given his name). Once the story resumes, on the other side of the 'sandwich', it sounds as though it's all much too late; but Jesus is quite confident, ignoring the jeers of those who refuse to believe him, and effortlessly (as always) performs the cure, commands them to silence (this command is unlikely to be obeyed, we feel), and charmingly exhorts them to feed the child.

In what ways do these stories shed light upon each other?

An unsuccessful return home

6 1-6 And he comes to his homeland. And they followed him, his disciples. And
when a Sabbath arrived, he began to teach in the synagogue. And many [people]

hearing were astounded, saying, 'From where [have] these things [come] to this [fellow]? And what is the wisdom that has been given to this [fellow], and such great miracles that happen through his hands? Is not this [fellow] the builder, the son of Mary and the brother of James and of Joses and of Judas and of Simon? And are not his sisters here with us?' And they were shocked by him. And Jesus said to them, 'A prophet is only dishonoured in his homeland, and among his kinsfolk, and in his household.' And he could not do any miracle there, except that he laid hands on a few sick [people] and healed them. And he was amazed on account of their unbelief.

We might expect a ticker-tape parade ('local boy makes good'); but we already know that Jesus is different. Not many people in the Gospel so far have really understood him, and his hometown continues the pattern: they are 'shocked' or 'scandalised' by him. So he can't do much in the way of miracles.

What does this tell us about Jesus?

Another 'sandwich': the apostles are sent out; John the Baptist is decapitated

7-32 And he went round the villages in a circle, teaching. And he summons the twelve. And he began to send them two by two, and he gave them authority [over] unclean spirits. And he directed them not to take anything for the way, except only a staff: 'No bread, no begging-bag, no copper for the belt: just have sandals tied on. And don't put on two tunics.' And he said to them, 'Wherever you go into a house, stay there until you come out from there. And whatever place does not receive you or listen to you, marching out from there shake the dust from under your feet as a witness to them.'

And they went out and proclaimed that [people] should repent. And they threw out many demons, and they anointed many sick people with oil and cured them.

And King Herod heard; for his name had become known. And he said, 'John the baptiser has risen from the dead, and that's the reason these miracles are at work in him.' And some [people] said, 'It's Elijah', and others said, 'A prophet, like one of the prophets'. But Herod was saying, when he heard, 'That [fellow] I decapitated: John – he has risen.' For Herod himself had sent and arrested John and tied him up in gaol, on account of Herodias, Philip his brother's wife, because he had married her. For John was telling Herod, 'You have no authority to have your brother's woman.'

And Herodias had it in for him, and she wanted to kill him. And she couldn't, for Herod was afraid of John, knowing him for a just man and a saint. And he protected him, and when he was listening to him he was deeply puzzled. And he used to listen to him gladly.

And when a good chance arrived, when Herod threw a banquet on his birthday for his magnates and his kiliarchs, and the Number Ones of the Galilee, and when his daughter Herodias came in and danced, she pleased Herod and those who lay down to dine with him. The king said to the little girl, 'Ask me whatever you want, and I shall give [it] to you.' And he swore to her, 'Whatever you ask me, I shall give you, "even unto half of my kingdom".' And going out, she said to her mother, 'What shall I ask for?'

And she said, 'The head of John the baptiser.'

And immediately going in with haste to the king, she asked him, saying, 'I want you to give me, straightaway, on a dish, the head of John the Baptist.'

And the king [although] becoming very sad, because of the oaths, and because of those who lay down [to dine], did not wish to thwart her. And immediately, the king, sending a scout, ordered him to bring his head. And going off he decapitated him in the prison. And he brought his head on the dish. And he gave it to the little girl. And the little girl gave it to her mother.

And hearing it his disciples came and took up his corpse and placed it in a tomb.

And the apostles gathered to Jesus and announced to him all the things that they had done and that they had taught.

And he says to them, 'Come here, you yourselves, privately, to a deserted place and refresh yourselves for a little.' For those who were coming and going were many, and they didn't even have a chance to eat. And they went in the boat to a deserted place, privately.

We have watched Jesus going about his mission; now it is the turn of the Twelve. Just like him, they are to have authority over unclean spirits; and they are to travel light, and (like Jesus) to expect rejection. Eventually they will return, full of all that they have done; but while they are away Mark invites us, by way of another 'sandwich', to reflect on the form which that rejection might take. The story of John the Baptist's death is a horrid one, with lively narrative and deftly drawn characters. Incidentally, the two women here are the only ones (in contrast to the blundering males) in Mark's Gospel who get things wrong. We may reflect that discipleship is not going to be easy.

'Even unto half my kingdom' is from Esther 5:3,6, where the speaker is another unpredictable tyrant addressing a woman from his household.

A hungry crowd (five thousand of them) taught and fed

33-44 And many saw them going and recognised [them/it?], and on foot, from all the cities, they ran there together. And they got there before them.

And going out he saw a great crowd and had pity on them, because they were 'like sheep who have no shepherd', and he began to teach them many things. And when it was already very late, his disciples coming to him said, 'The place is deserted, and it's already late. Dismiss them, so that they can go to the estates and villages about and buy for themselves something to eat.' He replied and said to them, 'Give them something to eat yourselves.' And they say to him, ' [You want us to] go off and buy loaves for two hundred denarii and give them to eat?'

But he says to them, 'How many loaves have you got? Go and see.' And they found out and say, 'Five. And two fishes.' And he instructed them to make everyone lie down in picnic-groups, on the green grass. And they lay down group by group, by fifty and a hundred. And taking the five loaves and the two fish, and looking up to heaven, he blessed and broke the loaves and gave to [his] disciples for them to place before them, and the two fish he divided for all. And they all ate and were filled. And they took up fragments, twelve full baskets, and also from the fish. And those who ate were five thousand men.

The disciples have returned from their missionary expedition, all ready for debriefing; but the crowds have their eye on Jesus, and there will be no privacy. Worse still (from the disciples' point of view) Jesus actually cares about these crowds. The disciples try to break it up, by looking at their watches and talking about food; but instead are told 'feed them yourselves'. They treat this suggestion with derision, but, in the end, feed them is precisely what they do.

'Like sheep without a shepherd' comes from Numbers 27:17 and Ezekiel 34:5. Both these texts are about how leadership should be exercised in Israel.

'Courage, IT IS I'

45-52 And immediately he compelled his disciples to embark on the boat and to go ahead to the other side, to Bethsaida, while he dismisses the crowd. And having said farewell, he went off to the mountain to pray. And when it grew late, the boat was in mid-sea; and he was alone on the land. And seeing them in distress in their rowing, for the wind was against them, around the fourth watch of the night he comes to them, walking on the sea. And he wanted to pass them by. But they, seeing him walking on the sea, thought that it was a ghost. And they cried out. For they all saw [him] and were disturbed. But he immediately spoke with them, and says to them, 'Courage, IT IS I.' And he came up to them, into the boat, and the wind abated. And they were exceedingly beside themselves in themselves. For they had not understood about the loaves. Instead, their heart was hardened.

Who is Jesus? Who are his disciples? Jesus effortlessly feeds five thousand people, and then needs to go and pray. The disciples are sent off by boat, but meet with difficulty, and Jesus approaches them, out of compassion. They are in no way comforted; instead, they are convinced that they are being haunted. Jesus replies 'It is I', which might just mean 'It's me, Jesus'; but it also echoes what God said at the burning bush in Exodus 3:14. For the first time, we are told clearly that the disciples fail to understand; and Mark applies to them the alarming phrase, 'their hearts were hardened'.

Could this phrase apply to us?

A summary of Jesus' activities

53-56 And crossing to the land they came to Gennesaret, and they docked. And when they disembarked, immediately recognising him they ran round that whole region, and they began to carry around on mattresses those who were in a bad way, wherever they heard that he was. And wherever he would journey, into villages or into towns or into fields, they placed the sick in the market places, and they begged him, that they might touch even the hem of his garment, and whoever touched him, were being saved.

Mark brings this chain of linked stories to an end now, by docking at Gennesaret; and, once again, Jesus is beset by the crowds, who long to be healed by him (and they are not disappointed). Notice how Mark leaves us to work out for ourselves who 'they' are in each sentence.

More disagreements on appropriate religious behaviour

7 1-23 And they came together to him, the Pharisees and some of the scribes coming from Jerusalem, and seeing some of his disciples, that with unclean (that is, unwashed) hands they eat loaves. For the Pharisees and all the Jews unless they have washed with the fist, do not eat, keeping a grip on the tradition of the elders, and [coming back] from the market place don't eat unless they have washed, and many other things which they have received to keep, washings of cups and jugs and bronzes. And the Pharisees and the scribes interrogate him, 'Why do your disciples not walk according to the tradition of the elders, but with unclean hands eat bread?'

And he said to them, 'It was well that Isaiah prophesied about you fakes [literally, 'actors'] as it is written:

"This people honours me with [their] lips,
but their heart is distant from me.
In vain do they worship me,
teaching teachings [which are] the instructions of humans."

'Abandoning the command of God, you hold firm to the tradition of human beings.'

And he said to them, 'Do you do well to nullify the command of God, so as to set up your tradition? For Moses said, "Honour your father and your mother"; and "The one who bad-mouths father or mother, let them die the death." You, on the other hand, say, "If a person says to [their] father or mother, 'Qorban,' (that is, gift) 'whatever you should have had from me.' " – you no longer let a person do anything for [their] father or mother, thus invalidating the word of your God by your tradition which you have traditioned. And you do many similar such things.'

And calling the crowd again, he was telling them, 'Listen to me all of you, and understand. There is nothing outside the person which comes into them which can make them unclean. Rather the things that come out of the person are those which make them unclean.'

And when he went into the house away from the crowd, his disciples asked him about the parable. And he says to them, 'So you too are unintelligent. Don't you understand that everything that from outside comes into the person cannot make them unclean? Because it does not come into the heart, but into their belly, and goes out into the latrine' (making all foods clean). But he went on to say, 'What comes out of the person, that is what makes the person unclean. For from within, from people's heart, come evil thoughts: fornications, thefts, murders, adulteries, greeds, wickednesses, debauchery, evil eye, blasphemy, arrogance, and foolishness. All these wicked things come out from inside, and make the person unclean.'

Once again we witness an encounter between Jesus and 'the Pharisees and some of the scribes coming from Jerusalem'. We know now that this means disagreement; and it must be said that Jesus' opponents have a point, when they observe his disciples' behaviour (though we have no idea what 'washing with the fist' might mean). When Jesus is criticised on religious grounds, he tends to quote Scripture, as he does here (Isaiah 29:13); for Jesus what counts is nothing else than doing the will of God, and he argues that his opponents tend to evade that will. He then sums up his message to the crowds, and, perhaps a little irritably, explains the matter to his not very sharp disciples.

'Qorban' is a Hebrew word, a gift consecrated to God, and therefore unavailable for charitable purposes.

Is there anything in the tradition of your Church that seems to go against the scriptures?

A woman whose retort changed Jesus' mind

24-30 Rising up from there he went off to the boundaries of Tyre. And going into a
house he wanted no one to know. And he could not pass unnoticed. Instead, immediately a woman heard about him, whose daughter had an unclean spirit, and came and
fell at his feet. Now the woman was a Greek-speaker, Syro-Phoenician by race. And
she asked him that he would cast the demon out of her daughter.

And he started to say to her, 'First let the children eat their fill. For it is not good to
take the children's loaf and fling it to little dogs.' And she replied and says to him,
'Lord, even the little dogs eat under the table, from the children's crumbs.' And he
said to her, 'Because of this remark, go; the demon has come out of your daughter.'
And going into her house she found her little child hurled on the bed, and the demon
gone out.

This is an extraordinary episode. Jesus retreats to non-Jewish territory, perhaps a little dispirited by inner-religious arguments, and meets a non-Jew who wants a favour, the healing of her daughter. His response is dismissive, and not apparently very polite, referring to Gentile women as 'little dogs'; but she maintains her cool, and wittily twists his words, apparently delighting Jesus so much that she gets her way. This Gospel is full of surprises.

How many times has the Gospel surprised you?

'He has done everything well'

31-37 And again going out of the boundaries, he came through Sidon into the Sea of
Galilee, up the middle of the boundaries of [the] Decapolis.

And they bring to him a deaf man with a speech impediment, and they beg him to
lay his hands on him. And taking him away from the crowd in private he put his fingers
into his ears, and, spitting, touched his tongue. And looking up to heaven he groaned,
and says to him, 'Ephphatha', which is 'Be opened'. And his ears were opened. And the
chain of his tongue was untied. And he started to talk properly. And he commanded

them that they tell nobody. But as much as he tried to command them, they proclaimed [it] all the more extravagantly. And they were super-extravagantly amazed, saying, 'He has done everything well: even the deaf he makes to hear, and speechless ones to speak.'

This episode also takes place in non-Jewish territory, but on the east rather than the west side, across the Jordan. As always, the healing is effortless; as so often there is the command to silence; and we are given Jesus' word in perfectly correct Aramaic. The point of the story may be in the echo of the Old Testament (see Isaiah 35:5, 6): Jesus is everything that Scripture had led us to expect. We recall the disciples' awed question at the end of Chapter 4: 'Who is this, that even the winds and the seas obey him?'

Feeding of the four thousand, and a reflection on failures to understand (hardening of the heart)

8 1-21 In those days again, there being a great crowd, and them not having anything to eat, summoning his disciples he says to them, 'I have compassion on the crowd, because for three whole days they stick with me, and they do not have anything to eat. And if I dismiss them fasting to their home, they will dissolve on the road. And some of them have come from a long way off.' And his disciples replied to him, 'From where will someone be able so to fill these people with loaves in the desert?' And he was asking them, 'How many loaves do you have?' And they said, 'Seven.'

And he commands the crowd to lie down on the ground. And taking the seven loaves he gave thanks and broke and gave to his disciples for them to place before [the people]. And they placed [them] before the crowd. And they had a few little fishes. And he blessed them and he said to place [them] also before. And they ate and were filled, and they took up surplus fragments, seven hampers. They were about four thousand. And he dismissed them.

And immediately he went on to the boat with his disciples, and came to the parts of Dalmanutha. And the Pharisees came out and began to contend with him, seeking from him a sign from heaven. They were testing him. And groaning in his spirit he says, 'Why does this generation seek a sign? Amen I say to you: no sign will be given to this generation [literally: 'if a sign shall be given to this generation…'].' And abandoning them he embarked again and went off to the other side. And they had forgotten to bring loaves. And they only had one with them in the boat. And he instructed, saying, 'Look, keep a watchful eye out against the leaven of the Pharisees and the leaven of Herod.' And they discussed with each other, because they don't have loaves. And knowing [what they were up to] he says to them, 'Why are you discussing that you don't have loaves? Do you neither understand nor comprehend? You have your heart hardened. Having eyes, do you not see, and having ears do you not hear?

'And don't you remember, when I broke the five loaves for the five thousand, how many baskets full of fragments you took up?' They said, 'Twelve.'

'When [I broke] the seven [loaves] for the four thousand, how many hampers full did you take up?' They tell him, 'Seven.'

And he says to them, 'Do you not yet understand?'

> *The point of this story, which in many respects echoes that earlier story where five thousand were fed, lies apparently in the obtuseness of Jesus' disciples. The seven loaves and a few fishes are made to stretch out so that not only does everyone eat, but there are seven hampers of surplus food. The story is briefly told, but really seems to set up a contrast between Jesus and a) the Pharisees (who want a sign) and b) the disciples (who have not only forgotten to bring a picnic, but also have no real notion what is going on). Jesus speaks of their inability to see, echoing Jeremiah 5:21 and Ezekiel 12:2.*
>
> *The question is therefore forcefully addressed to the reader: do* **you** *understand?*

The start of Jesus' instruction of his disciples

22-26 And they came to Bethsaida. And they bring to him a blind man and they beg him to touch him. And taking the hand of the blind man, he took him outside the village. And spitting into his eyes he laid his hands on him and asked him, 'Do you see anything?' And recovering his sight [or: looking up] he said, 'I am looking at human beings, because I see them walking like trees.' Then again he laid hands on his eyes. And he saw clearly and was restored, and he beheld everything plainly. And he sent him to his home, saying, 'Don't even go into the village.'

> *We have established that the disciples do not understand very much. Now comes a period when they are being instructed, especially about the fact that Jesus must die. This time of instruction starts with the present story, and ends at 10:46-52. In other words, the whole instruction period is framed by two stories in which blind men have their sight restored; perhaps this symbolises what happens to Jesus' disciples in the course of the instruction.*
>
> *This particular healing is unusual: Jesus leads the blind man away privately; he spits into his eyes; the miracle is initially only partially successful ('I see them walking like trees') – and then the cured man is told to go home, 'not even into the village'. All this may symbolise where the disciples are just at present.*
>
> *Where are* **you** *just at present?*

Caesarea Philippi: a Messiah who will suffer (and has disciples who don't understand)

8[27]-9[1] And Jesus went out, and his disciples, to the villages of Caesarea Philippi. And on the way he interrogated his disciples saying to them, 'Who do people say I am?' And they told him, saying, 'John the Baptist. And others Elijah, and others that [you are] one of the prophets.'

And he himself interrogated them, 'Now you: who do you yourselves say I am?' Peter replied and says to him, 'You are the Messiah.' And he scolded them, to tell nobody about him.

And he began to teach them that it was necessary for the Son of Man to suffer many things, and to be rejected by the elders and the high priests and the scribes, and to be killed, and after three days rise again. And he said the message openly. And Peter, taking him aside, began to scold him. And he turned, and, seeing his disciples, scolded Peter and says, 'Get behind me, Satan. Because you are not thinking God's thoughts but human thoughts.' And summoning the crowd with his disciples he said to them, 'If someone wants to follow after me, let them deny themselves, and take up their cross, and follow me. For whoever wants to save their life will destroy it. And whoever destroys their life, for my sake and for the sake of the gospel, will save it. For what use is it for a person to gain the entire world and suffer the loss of their life? For what would a person give in exchange for their life? For whoever is ashamed of me and of my words in this adulterous and sinful generation, the Son of Man will also be ashamed of him when he comes in his Father's glory with the holy angels.' And he was telling them, 'Amen I say to you: there are some of those who stand here who will not taste death until they see the kingdom of God coming in power.'

This central passage continues the theme of the disciples' education; the process seems to be a combination of light dawning and dark incomprehension. It starts with a survey of current views ('Who do people say I am?'), then moves to an uncomfortably direct question: 'Who do you yourselves say I am?' Peter gets it stunningly right; but then, when the implications of his answer are unfolded, stunningly wrong, for he cannot cope with a Messiah who is to be killed. And so he is, for his pains, addressed as 'Satan'. It is important for disciples to understand this business of a Messiah who has to die. Disciples have to be prepared to imitate their master, right to the end.

Who do **you** *say Jesus is? And what must his disciples be like?*

Continuing education: the Transfiguration

2-13 And six days later Jesus takes aside Peter and James and John and carries them up to a high mountain privately, on their own. And he was transformed before them, and his garments became radiant, very white such as a bleacher on earth could not so whiten [them]. And there appeared to them Elijah with Moses; and they were talking together with Jesus. And Peter responded and says to Jesus, 'Rabbi, it is good for us to be here. And let's make three tents, one for you, and one for Moses and one for Elijah.'

For he had no idea how to respond. For they became terrified. And there came a cloud overshadowing them; and there came a voice from the cloud, 'This is my Son, the beloved. Listen to him.'

And suddenly, looking round, they no longer saw anybody, except Jesus, on his own, with them.

And as they came down out of the mountain, he instructed them that they should narrate to nobody what they had seen, except when the Son of Man should be risen from the dead. And they hung on to the message for themselves, arguing what 'rising from the dead' was. And they interrogated him, saying, 'The scribes say that Elijah has to come first.' And he said to them, 'Elijah indeed comes first, and restores everything. And how is it written about the Son of Man that he should suffer a great deal and be treated with contempt? But I tell you that Elijah has come, and they did to him as they pleased, as it is written about him.'

The instruction of the disciples goes on, although here it is only his 'inner cabinet', Peter, James and John, who are given their instructions. Up the mountain, two things happen: first, Jesus is 'transfigured', and whatever we make of this, it is clearly intended as a glimpse of the truth about him. Second, Jesus is seen chatting with Elijah and Moses, the Prophets and the Law, so that he is at least the equal of them. Then Peter blows it, with his willing but not very sensible suggestion of building a camping-site. Notice that 'they became terrified'. This is the sign of the presence of God; and, sure enough, there is a cloud and the voice of God, confirming what we heard at the Baptism (1:11), 'This is my Son, the beloved', with the instruction (which they will do well to observe), 'listen to him'.

With these words ringing in their ears they go down the mountain. Then they (and we) are told that this can't be understood until Jesus is raised from the dead, and are invited to think about Elijah. But they don't really understand very much.

Another failure by the disciples

14-29 And coming to the disciples they saw a great crowd about them, and scribes arguing against them. And immediately the whole crowd seeing him was amazed. And they ran up and greeted him. And he asked them, 'Why are you debating against them? And one of the crowd responded to him, 'Teacher, I brought my son to you, since he has a dumb spirit. And whenever it overtakes him, it dashes him to the ground and he foams at the mouth and gnashes his teeth and he becomes stiff. And I told your disciples that they should expel [the demon]. And they had not the strength.' He responded to them saying, 'O faithless generation! How long shall I be with you? How long shall I put up with you? Bring him to me.' And they brought him to him. And seeing him the spirit immediately convulsed him. And falling on the ground he rolled [about], foaming at the mouth. And he asked his father, 'How long a time is it that this has happened to him?' And he said, 'From since childhood. And often it threw him into a fire and into waters, to destroy him. But, if you can, help us, having compassion on us.' And Jesus said to him, 'That "If you can" – everything is possible to the one who believes.' Immediately, the father cried out and said, 'I believe: help my unbelief!' And Jesus, seeing that a crowd was running together, scolded the unclean spirit, saying to it, 'You dumb and deaf spirit, I command you, come out of him, and never enter into him again.' And crying out and convulsing him it came out. And he became just like a corpse, so that many said, 'He's dead!' But

Jesus gripped his hand and raised him up, and he stood up again [or: 'resurrected'].

And when he went into a [the?] house, his disciples asked him, 'Couldn't we cast it out?' And he said to them, 'This kind can't come out by any method but prayer.'

Now, as they rejoin the others, comes another failure. The disciples (presumably all but the three who were up the mountain) have been unable to heal a boy who was possessed by a demon, and the crowd and the boy's father clearly want 'the organ-grinder, not his monkeys'. There is more dialogue than we are used to, as Jesus discovers the circumstances, and twice emphasises the need for faith. Then the boy is healed, although not without a struggle, and the crowds thinking he was dead. The point of the story, however, seems to be the education of the disciples, puzzled at their failure – and Jesus simply stresses the need for prayer.

Do you need to pray more?

Continuing education: the Messiah and his disciples

30-50 And going out from there they went through the Galilee, and he did not want anyone to know. For he was teaching his disciples and telling them, 'The Son of Man is being handed over into human hands. And they'll kill him. And having been killed, after three days he will rise up.' And they didn't know the thing. And they were afraid to ask him. And they came to Caphernaum. And being in the house, he asked them, 'What were you discussing on the road?' But they were silent. For they had been discussing against each other on the road, 'Who's greatest?' And he sat down, and addressed the twelve and says to them, 'If someone wants to be Number One, they will be last of all and servant of all.'

And he took a little child and placed it in the middle of them. And taking it in his arms, he said to them, 'Whoever receives one such child as this in my name receives me. And whoever receives me receives not me but the one who sent me.'

John said to him, 'Teacher, we saw someone in your name casting out demons, and we stopped him, because he didn't follow us.' And Jesus said, 'Don't stop him. For there's no one who can do a miracle in my name and will then quickly be able to badmouth me. For whoever is not against us is on our side. For whoever gives you a drink of water because you belong to Messiah, Amen I tell you, no way will that person lose their reward. And whoever makes one of these little ones stumble, who believe in me, it is good for him rather if a millstone worked by a donkey is put round his neck and he has been thrown into the sea. And if your hand causes you to stumble, cut if off: it is better for you to go deformed into life than to go with two hands into Gehenna, into the unquenched fire. And if your foot causes you to stumble, cut it off. It is better for you to enter life lame than to have two feet and be thrown into Gehenna. And if your eye causes you to stumble, throw it away: it is better for you to enter one-eyed into the kingdom of God than with two eyes to be thrown into Gehenna, where their worm does not die and the fire is not extinguished. For everyone will be salted by fire. Salt is good: but if that salt becomes saltless, with what will you season it? Have salt in yourselves. And be at peace among each other.'

A second time now Jesus predicts his own death (the first time was in the previous chapter, at Caesarea Philippi); a second time the disciples show they don't understand a word. This time, however, it's different. First, Mark emphasises that this is just for disciples ('he did not want anyone to know, for he was teaching his disciples . . . '). Second, the disciples turn out to have been discussing who was Top Apostle. So they have to be educated, but still take no notice, for no sooner has the lesson ended than John is begging for Jesus to praise him for not allowing someone to cast out demons in Jesus' name. Jesus has to tell them that the only thing that matters is to belong to the kingdom of God.

Notice how Mark has built up the final paragraph, using teachings with three 'keywords': 'stumble' (or 'scandal'), 'fire', and 'salt'. That may help you to understand what can otherwise be a rather difficult passage.

Do you find Jesus' death hard to take?

Three controversies: Pharisees and divorce; the disciples on children; the rich man and eternal life

10 1-31 And from there rising up he comes to the regions of Judaea and across the Jordan, and crowds came together to him, and as he was accustomed, again he started to teach them. And Pharisees approached and asked him, 'Does a man have authority to send a woman away?', testing him. But he answering said to them, 'What did Moses command you?' They said, 'Moses allowed us to "draw up a certificate of divorce and send her away".' Jesus said to them, 'It was with regard to your hard-heartedness that he wrote down this commandment for you. But from the beginning of creation, "male and female he created them. For this reason a man shall leave his father and mother and stick to his wife, and the two shall turn into one flesh". So – what God has yoked together, let human beings not separate.'

And back in the house the disciples asked him about this. And he says to them, 'Whoever sends his woman away and marries another commits adultery on her; and if she sends her husband away and marries another, she commits adultery.'

And they were offering him children, for him to touch them; but the disciples scolded them. But when Jesus saw [it] he was angry, and he said to them, 'Allow the children to come to me. Don't stop them – for of such is the kingdom of God. Amen I say to you, whoever does not receive the kingdom of God like a child, no way will that person enter it.' And taking them in his arms he blessed them, laying hands on them.

And he was going out on to the road, running up one [person] and kneeling to him interrogated him, 'Good teacher, what shall I do in order that I may inherit eternal life?' But Jesus said to him, 'Why do you call me good? No one is good, except one, God. You know the commandments: "You shall not kill. You shall not commit adultery. You shall not steal. You shall not bear false witness. You shall not defraud. Honour your father and mother".' But he said to him, 'Teacher, all these things I have kept from my youth.' But Jesus fixed his gaze on him and loved him and said, 'One thing is missing for you. Go – whatever you have, sell it and give to the poor. And you will have treasure in heaven. And come here, follow me.'

But he was appalled at this remark and went off grieving. For he was a man who had many possessions. And looking around, Jesus says to his disciples, 'With what difficulty will those who have [material] things enter the kingdom of God.' And his disciples were astounded at his remarks. But Jesus again answering says to them, 'Children, how difficult it is to enter the kingdom of God. It is easier for a camel to go through the eye of a needle than for a rich person to enter the kingdom of God.' But they were overwhelmed beyond measure, saying to themselves, 'And who can be saved?' Fixing his gaze on them, Jesus says, 'For humans it's impossible, but not for God. You see, everything is possible for God.' Peter began to say to him, 'Look! We have abandoned everything, and have followed you.' Jesus says, 'Amen I say to you, there is no one who has abandoned home or brothers or sisters or mother or father or children or fields because of me and because of the gospel, but they will receive a hundredfold now in this time – houses and brothers and sisters and mothers and children and fields (along with persecutions) – and in the coming world, eternal life. You see, many first will be last, and last first.'

Another rather vague geographical introduction presents us with crowds and with Pharisees. The Pharisees ask an important question about when divorce is admissible. Jesus' answer is 'never'. The disciples are baffled by this, and also by his willingness to bless children; then an over-pious and over-affluent questioner interrogates him about eternal life. He goes off sad at the answer Jesus gives him. This in turn sows alarm and despondency among the disciples, and Peter. Finally Jesus gives them a clue about the mystery of discipleship: disciples 'will receive a hundredfold'.

Notice that Jesus and his interlocutors agree on the Old Testament as their starting-point: on marriage (Genesis 1:27; 2:24) and on the question of divorce (Deuteronomy 24:1-4).

Do you find that Jesus gets easier or harder to understand, as the Gospel goes on?

More failure on the part of the disciples

32-45 Now they were on the road going up to Jerusalem, and Jesus was leading them [or: going before them], and they were astounded, and those who followed were afraid. And again taking the twelve he began to tell them the things that were about to happen to him: 'Look! We are going up to Jerusalem, and the Son of Man will be handed over to the high priests and to the scribes. And they will condemn him to death, and they will hand him over to Gentiles. And they will mock him, and they'll spit on him, and they'll whip him. And they will kill him. And after three days he will rise.'

And up to him come James and John, the sons of Zebedee, saying to him, 'Teacher, we want you to do for us whatever we ask you.' And he said to them, 'What do you want me to do for you?' And they said to him, 'Grant us that we should sit in your glory, one on your right and one on your left.' But Jesus said to them, 'You do not know what you are asking. Can you drink the cup that I drink? Or can you be baptised [in] the baptism [with] which I am to be baptised?' But they told him, 'We can.' But Jesus told them, 'The cup that I drink you will drink. And the baptism [with] which I am being baptised you shall be baptised. But to sit on the right or on the left is not mine to give; but it is [for those] for whom it has been prepared.' And hearing this, the ten began to be annoyed about James and John. And summoning them Jesus says to them, 'You know that those who think they rule the Gentiles dominate them. And their great ones exercise authority over them. Not so is it among you. Instead, whoever wants to be Number One among you will be everyone's slave. You see, the Son of Man did not come to be served, but to serve. And to give [his] life [as] a ransom for many.'

A third time Jesus explains to his disciples about his imminent death, and a third time they show that they have not understood a word. Notice how Mark sets it up: the road to Jerusalem (where we already know that he is going to die), and the fact that they were 'astounded' and 'afraid', all of this makes our mood quite sombre by the time Jesus actually starts talking about his suffering and death. Then the sons of Zebedee try and get in ahead of the rest, and have to be told, 'It's not like that'; and when the other ten start to get cross, they also have to be educated. So, linking discipleship to what Jesus is like, or to who Jesus is, we are told, with a clarity that we shall do well to heed, 'You see, the Son of Man did not come to be served, but to serve. And to give [his] life [as] a ransom for many.'

Bartimaeus: a disciple who gets it right

46-52 And they come to Jericho. And as he is going out of Jericho, and his disciples, and a fair old crowd, the son of Timaeus, Bartimaeus, a blind beggar, was sitting by the road. And hearing that it was Jesus the Nazarene, he began to cry out and say, 'Son of David, Jesus, have mercy on me.' And many people scolded him, that he should be silent. But he cried out much more, 'Son of David, have mercy on me.' And Jesus stood, and said, 'Call him.' And they call the blind man, telling him, 'Courage! Arise. He is calling you.' And he threw off his cloak, leapt up, and came to Jesus. Jesus responded to him and said, 'What do you want me to do for you?' And the blind man said to him, 'Rabbouni, that I may see again.' And Jesus said to him, 'Go. Your faith has saved you.' And immediately he saw again. And he followed him on the road.

This section of the Gospel began with one blind man being healed, and ends with another. We are invited to admire this one's persistence, despite the scolding of the people around him; we are cheered when Jesus summons him, perhaps a little alarmed as he strips off his clothes and blunders sightless through the crowd. Then he expresses clearly, and with absolute confidence, what he wants: 'that I may see again' – calling Jesus 'Rabbouni' as he does so. Finally, this man who had been 'by the road' at the beginning of the story now 'followed him on the road'. He has become a disciple, and is cheerfully following Jesus, even though the road leads to Jerusalem and to death.

Jesus finally enters Jerusalem

11 1-11 And when they drew nearer to Jerusalem, to Bethphage and Bethany, towards the Mountain of Olives, he sends two of his disciples and says to them, 'Go into the village that is opposite you. And immediately when you go into it you will find a colt tied up, on which no human being has ever sat. Untie it and bring it. And if someone says to you, "Why are you doing this?", say, "The Lord has need of it and he will send it back here immediately."' And they went off and found the colt tied at a door outside on the street. And they untie it. And some of those standing there started to say to them, 'What are you doing, untying the colt?' But they said to them as Jesus had said. And they let them go. And they take the colt to Jesus and they threw their cloaks on it; and he sat on it. And many people spread their cloaks on the road. And others [were] cutting leafy branches from the fields. And those who went before and those who followed cried out,

'Hosanna! Blessed the one who comes in the name of the Lord.
Blessed the coming kingdom of our father David!
Hosanna in the Highest!'

And he went into Jerusalem, into the Temple. And looking around at everything, the hour being already late, he went out to Bethany with the Twelve.

It has been a while coming, and our mood is now a bit grim, but here we are, on the outskirts of Jerusalem, the desert side, from which the Messiah was supposed to come. Jesus has it all under control, gives instructions for hijacking a donkey (one that is not used to being ridden, alarmingly enough). The procession goes ahead uneventfully, with cloaks and branches and a quotation from Psalm 118 (verses 25, 26, but read through the whole psalm, and remember that 'Hosanna' is the Hebrew for 'please save us'); and Jesus arrives in the Temple without being thrown by his beast of burden.

This has been an odd Gospel all the way through, and at this moment of apparent climax it does not cease to be so, for the Messiah comes triumphantly to Jerusalem, enters the Temple (as you would expect) and then, just as we are waiting for him to deliver independence and send the occupying Roman forces back into the sea, with an extraordinary sense of anti-climax he merely looks about the place and retires to Bethany!

The Temple and the fig tree

12-25 And on the next day, when they were coming from Bethany he was hungry. And seeing from a long way off a fig tree with leaves, he went to see if he should find anything on it. And coming to it he found nothing on it but leaves (for it was not the season for figs). And in response he said to it, 'No longer, for ever, may anyone eat fruit from you.' And his disciples heard.

And they came to Jerusalem. And going into the Temple he began to throw out those who sold and bought in the Temple. And the tables of the moneychangers and the seats of those who sold doves, he simply overturned. And he did not allow anyone to carry a vessel through the Temple. And he was teaching and telling them, 'Is it not written, "My house shall be called a house of prayer for all the Gentiles"? And you have made it a cave of brigands.' And the chief priests and the scribes heard. And they sought how they might destroy him. For they were afraid of him; for the whole crowd was overwhelmed at his teaching. And when it grew late they went outside the city.

And early in the morning as they went by, they saw the fig tree, withered from the roots. And, remembering, Peter says to him, 'Rabbi, look! The fig tree you cursed has withered!' And Jesus answering says to him, 'Have faith [in] God. Amen I tell you, whoever says to this mountain, "Be lifted up and be thrown into the sea", and does not doubt in their heart but believes that what they say is happening, it will be theirs. Therefore I tell you, everything that you pray and ask for, believe that you received it, and it will be yours.

'And whenever you stand praying, let it go if you have anything against anybody, so that your Father, the one in heaven, may let go of your transgressions for you.'

This is an episode which has always puzzled readers. It is better, though, to see it as **two** *episodes. Jesus' cursing of the fig tree often seems uncomfortably petulant, especially as 'it was not the season for figs'; but take the fig tree as a symbol of Israel, see the Temple as that which should always have borne fruit, whatever the season, if people had only been open to God, and it all starts to fall into place. What counts here is the Temple, which has become a shopping-mall ('cave of brigands') instead of 'a house of prayer' (Jesus here quotes Isaiah 56:7). For Jesus, the central relationship is his intimacy with the God whom he calls 'Father'; get that right, and Temples will be what they should be, the nation will bear fruit, and extraordinary things will start to happen; we may even learn to forgive one another.*

Does the story of the fig tree make you feel uncomfortable?

Clashes with religious leaders about 'authority'

11[27]–12[44] And they came again to Jerusalem. And as he was walking in the Temple the high priests and the scribes and the elders come to him, and they began to say to him, 'By what authority do you do these things? Or who gave you this authority that you should do these things?' And Jesus said to them, 'I shall ask you one thing; and you can answer me. And [then] I'll tell you by what authority I do these things. The baptism of John: was it from heaven or from human beings? Answer me.' And they argued among themselves, saying 'If we say, "From heaven", he'll say, "So why didn't you believe him?" But if we say, "From human beings . . . ".' (They were afraid of the crowd, for they all regarded John as really a prophet.) And they responded to Jesus, 'We don't know.' And Jesus says to them, 'Nor am I telling you by what authority I am doing these things.'

And he began to speak in parables, 'A man planted a vineyard; and he put a hedge round, and dug a trough, and built a tower. And he leased it to [tenant-] farmers, and went overseas. And at the season he sent a slave to the tenants, to accept some of the fruit of the vineyard from them. And they took him and flogged him and sent him away with nothing. And a second time he sent them another slave. This one they struck on the head and insulted. He sent a third slave. This one they killed, along with many others, some of whom they flogged, and others they killed. He still had one [resource?], a beloved son. He sent him last of all, saying, "They will have respect for my son." But those tenants said to themselves, "This is the heir. Come, let us kill him; and ours will be the inheritance." And they took him and killed him and flung him out of the vineyard. So what will the master of the vineyard do? He will come and destroy the tenants. And he will give the vineyard to others. Have you never even read the scripture,

"A stone which the builders rejected,
this became the cornerstone.
This came from the Lord
and it is wonderful in our eyes"?'

And they sought to arrest him; and they feared the crowd. For they knew that it was in respect of them he told the parable. And abandoning him they went off. And they send to him some of the Pharisees and the Herodians, to catch him out verbally. And they come and say to him, 'Teacher, we know that you are for real, and you're not bothered about anybody, because you don't worry about people's status, but in truth you teach God's way. Is it authorised to pay poll tax to Caesar or not? Do we give it or not give it?' But he knew they were putting on an act, and he said, 'Why do you test me? Bring me a denarius, for me to look at.' They did so, and he says to them, 'Whose image and inscription is this?' And they said to him, 'Caesar's.' And Jesus said to them, 'What belongs to Caesar, pay to Caesar. And what belongs to God, pay it to God.' And they wondered greatly at him.

And Sadducees came to him, people who say there is no such thing as Resurrection. And they interrogated him, saying, 'Teacher, Moses wrote for us that if someone's brother dies and leaves a wife and he doesn't leave a child, then his brother should take his wife and raise up seed for his brother. There were seven brothers: and the first took a wife, and when he died he left no seed. So the second took her, and died, leaving no seed, and the third likewise. All seven left no seed. Last of all, the woman died. In the Resurrection, of which of them will she be the wife? For [all] seven had her as wife.' Jesus said to them, 'Is this not the reason that you go astray, that you do not know the scriptures or the power of God? For when they rise from the dead, they do not marry, nor are they given in marriage; instead, they are like angels in heaven. But with regard to the dead, for evidence that they are raised, did you not read in Moses' book, at the bush, how God told him, saying "I [am] the God of Abraham and the God of Isaac and the God of Jacob"? God is not God of corpses, but of the living. You are badly astray.'

And approaching, one of the scribes, hearing them argue, seeing that he had made a good answer to them, asked him, 'Which commandment is first of all?' Jesus replied, 'Number One is, "Hear, O Israel, the Lord our God is one Lord"; and "You will love the Lord your God out of your whole heart and your whole soul and your whole understanding and your whole strength." This is the second: "You will love your neighbour as yourself." Greater than these there is no other commandment.' And the scribe said to him, 'Beautifully [spoken], Teacher. Truly you said that [God] "is one and there is no other except for God". And "loving God out of one's whole heart and whole intelligence and whole strength" and "loving one's neighbour as oneself" is greater than all holocausts and sacrifices.' And Jesus, seeing that he replied thoughtfully, replied [and] said to him, 'You are not far from the kingdom of God.'

And no one dared any longer to interrogate him.

And in response Jesus was saying as he taught in the Temple, 'How do the scribes say that the Messiah is the son of David? You see, David himself said in the Holy Spirit,

"The Lord said to my Lord:
Sit at my right
until I place your enemies beneath your feet."

'David himself calls [Messiah] "Lord", so how come [Messiah] is his son?' And the crowd used to listen to him with delight.

And in his teaching he was saying, 'Look away from the scribes who want to walk about in long robes, and [who want] greetings in market places, and front-row seats in synagogues, and Number One spots at banquets. These people who devour the houses of widows, and make a pretence of praying for a long time: they are the ones who will receive an overwhelming judgement.'

And sitting opposite the Treasury, he was gazing at how the crowd threw their change into the Treasury. And lots of wealthy people put in lots. Then there came a single destitute widow-woman: and she threw in two tiny [coins], a farthing.

And summoning his disciples, he told them, 'Amen I tell you: this widow, the destitute woman, threw more than all who threw [money] into the Treasury. You see, they all threw [in] from their surplus. But she, from her poverty, threw [in] everything she had, her whole life.'

The episode where Jesus threw the money-changers out of the Temple raised questions about Jesus' 'authority', an issue that has been present since the beginning of the Gospel; and now the quarrel is out in the open. It starts with an attempt to trap Jesus, which he easily turns back on his opponents, adding for good measure the parable of the vineyard, which obviously echoes Isaiah 5:1-7 ('the vineyard of the Lord of Hosts is the House of Israel'), but also clearly foreshadows Jesus' own death at his opponents' hands.

Then comes a lethal trap, set by the unlikely combination of Herodians and Pharisees whom we have seen before (3:6), about the poll tax. Jesus easily sidesteps the trap, only to be assailed by yet another group, the Sadducees, trying to demonstrate the absurdity of belief in Resurrection. Not for the first time, Jesus uses the Torah to combat their own use of it (Exodus 3:6).

Next comes what at first sight looks like yet another attack on him, concerning the difficult question of which commandment is the most important, but it turns into a most unexpected and warming meeting of minds, as Jesus and the scribe discover that they are speaking the same language.

Once again it is worth noting that Jesus draws on his easy mastery of the Old Testament, quoting Deuteronomy 6:5 (which a prayerful Jew will say three times a day) and Leviticus 19:18.

Then Jesus goes on to the attack, demonstrating (from Scripture again, see Psalm 110:1) that the Messiah is actually David's Lord – and thereby making a claim that will certainly have annoyed his opponents. From there he delivers an aggressive warning about the 'scribes', whom we have increasingly, all through the Gospel, learnt to see as the enemy. And no sooner have we heard them dismissed as those who 'devour the houses of widows' than Jesus singles out precisely a poor widow as the most generous person in that very Temple where he has just made his outrageous prophetic gesture. She, and not the buyers and sellers, nor the religious people, is attentive to God.

The coming destruction

13 1-37 And as he was going out of the Temple, one of his disciples says to him, 'Teacher, look what stones, and what buildings!' And Jesus said to him, 'Do you see these great buildings? There will not be left here a stone upon a stone that will not be destroyed.'

And as he was sitting on the Mountain of Olives opposite the Temple, Peter and James and John and Andrew asked him privately, 'Tell us when these things will be, and what is the sign when all these things are about to be accomplished?' And Jesus began to say to them, 'Look out, that no one lead you astray. Many will come in my name, saying "I AM", and they will lead many astray. But when you hear of wars and rumours of wars, don't be frightened. It must happen, but the end [is] not yet. For nation shall be raised against nation and kingdom against kingdom. There shall be earthquakes in places; there will be famines. These things are the beginnings of [the] birth-pangs. But you, look at yourselves: they will betray you to Sanhedrins and Synagogues. You will be flogged, and you will be stood before procurators and kings, for my sake, as witness to them.

'And the gospel has first to be preached to all the nations. And when they take you, handing [you] over, don't get agitated beforehand [about] what you will say. Instead, whatever is given to you at that hour, say that. For it isn't you who are saying [it], but the Holy Spirit. And brother will hand over brother to death, and a father a child. And children will rebel against parents and put them to death. And you will be hated by all because of my name. But the one who endures to the end – that one will be saved.

'But when you see the abomination of desolation standing where it ought not (let the reader understand), then let those in Judaea flee into the mountains. Let the one [who is] on top of the house not come down, nor enter the house to take anything out. And the one who goes into the field, let him not turn back to take his cloak. Woe to women who are pregnant and who are suckling in those days. Pray that it doesn't happen in wintertime: for those days will be tribulation, such as has not occurred like this from the beginning of the creation which God created until now, and will not happen again. And if the Lord did not curtail the days, no flesh would be saved. But because of the chosen ones whom he chose he curtailed the days.

'And then, if anyone tells you, "Look! Here is the Messiah!" or "Look! There!" don't believe [them]. For there shall arise false Messiahs and false prophets and they shall give signs and portents, so as to lead astray, were it possible, even the chosen. But you see: I have predicted everything for you.

'But in those days after the tribulation,
the sun will be darkened
and the moon shall not give her light.
And the stars shall be falling from heaven
and the powers in the heavens shall totter.

'And then they shall see the Son of Man coming on clouds with much power and glory. And then he will send his angels, and he will gather together the chosen ones from the four winds, from the furthest point of the earth to the furthest point of heaven.

'From the fig tree learn the parable. When its branch now becomes tender and it puts forth leaves, you know that the summer [or: harvest] is near. So you, when you see these things happening, you know that he is close upon the gates. Amen I tell you, no way will this generation pass away until all these things happen. Heaven and earth shall pass away: but my words shall not pass away.

'But about that day or that hour no one knows, not even the angels in heaven, nor the Son, but only the Father. Look, stay awake. For you do not know when the time is. Like a man who went overseas, left his house and gave his slaves his authority, for each his own work, and instructed the gatekeeper to stay awake. So you stay awake. For you do not know when the Lord of the house comes, whether late in the day or in the middle of the night or at cockcrow or early in the morning. [Be careful] lest he come suddenly and find you sleeping. What I say to you I say to all: stay awake!'

This alarming and dramatic speech continues the mysterious discomfort that we have experienced throughout the Gospel. It starts with the naïve admiration of a spiritual tourist among the disciples, exclaiming over the beauty of Herod's Temple; but Jesus has twice already given his verdict on the Temple, and now he predicts its destruction. The 'inner cabinet' (plus Andrew, for once) asks him about the when and the how, but Jesus is prepared only to tell them that it will be tough, but that (also) all will be well, provided that they don't get too credulous. He quotes Isaiah 13:10 and 34:4 to give an idea of how dreadful it will all be, how unreliable all will seem to be that we have hitherto relied on. So we have to be alert for the signs, but not pretend to know too much: 'stay awake' is (literally) the watchword.

Introducing the Passion; another 'Marcan sandwich'

14 1-11 Now it was the Passover and Unleavened Bread after two days. And the high priests and the scribes were trying to see how they could arrest him by

stealth and kill him. For they were saying, 'Not at the festival, lest there be a popular riot.'

And while he was in Bethany at the house of Simon the leper, while he lay down to dine, there came a woman. She had an alabaster jar of myrrh, pistachio-nard, genuine and very expensive. She broke the alabaster jar and poured it over his head. And there were some people getting quietly indignant: 'To what end has this waste of myrrh taken place? For this myrrh could have been sold for more than three hundred denarii, and given to the poor.' And they snorted indignantly at her. But Jesus said, 'Leave her be. Why do you give her hassle? She has worked a good work in [regard to] me. For it is always the case that you have the poor with you; and whenever you want you can be bountiful to them. But me you do not always have. She has done what her resources allowed: she took an early opportunity to anoint my body for burial. But, Amen I tell you, wherever the gospel is preached in the whole world, even what she has done will be spoken of in remembrance of her.'

And Judas Iscariot (one of the Twelve) went off to the high priests to betray him to them. And when they heard they rejoiced; and they promised to give him money. And he started to look to see how he might betray him at an appropriate time.

Suddenly, with the imminence of the Passover (the first time that this great feast has been mentioned in the Gospel) we are rushing towards the end that we have seen coming for some time now. Mark introduces the story with one of his 'sandwiches'. He wraps the story of the high priests and scribes wanting to commit discreet homicide, and their finding a willing accomplice in Judas, round a quite different story, of the anointing at the house of Simon the leper. The woman who performs this unconventional action (presenting Jesus as Messiah) is clearly the story's heroine, her generosity contrasting with the murderous plans of the religious leaders and the treachery of Judas, and the small-mindedness of Jesus' fellow-guests. Hers is not the whole story, however, for Jesus gives another verdict on what she has done; she has anointed him for his 'burial'. These two stories, mixing generosity and love with some notably less attractive emotions, are Mark's way of telling us how to read the Passion Narrative.

A Passover meal gone wrong

12-25 And on the first day of Unleavened Bread, when they were sacrificing the Passover, his disciples said to him, 'Where do you want us to go and prepare for you to eat the Passover?' And he sends two of his disciples and says to them, 'Go into the city; and a man carrying a jar of water will meet you. Follow him. And wherever he enters, tell the master of the house, "The teacher says, 'Where is my lodging, where I may eat the Passover with my disciples?'." And he will show you a big upstairs room furnished and ready. And there prepare for us.'

And the disciples went out and went to the city; and they found [things] as he had said to them. And they prepared the Passover.

And when it grows late he comes with the Twelve. And as they lay down and were eating, Jesus said, 'Amen I say to you, one of you will betray me, the one who is eating with me.' They began to grieve, and to say to him, one by one, 'Surely it's not me, is it?' And he said to them, 'One of the Twelve, the one who dips his hand into the bowl with me. Because the Son of Man goes as it is written about him. But woe to that person through whom the Son of Man is handed over. It [would be] good for him if that person had not been born.'

And as they were eating, he took bread, blessed, broke, and gave it to them, and said, 'Take, this is my body.' And he took a cup and gave thanks, and gave it to them. And they all drank of it. And he said to them, 'This is my blood of the covenant. It is poured out for many. Amen I tell you that no way any longer shall I drink of the fruit of the vine until that day when I drink it new in the kingdom of God.'

After the sandwiched story of the anointing, we attend the Passover meal. This is the greatest and most joyous meal of the Jewish year, but our expectations are going to be disappointed. We note that in the crowded city of Jerusalem the disciples have only just wondered about making arrangements. Fortunately Jesus has already set something up on his own account. That, however, is the last piece of good news for a while, because no sooner has the meal begun than Jesus predicts that one of those sharing this great occasion with him will betray him, an almost unimaginable offence against the Near Eastern code of hospitality. Nor does the mood lift very much as he takes the bread and wine and says, 'This is my body . . . this is my blood of the covenant. It is poured out for many.' Whatever else this means, it sounds like death.

Gethsemani: idle boasting, and a desperately serious prayer

26-42 And they sang a hymn and went out to the Mountain of Olives. And Jesus said to them, 'You will all be led into sin, because it is written,

"I shall strike the shepherd
and the sheep shall be scattered."

'But after I have been raised I shall go before you [or: lead you] into Galilee.' And Peter said to him, 'Even if all [the others] are led into sin . . . but not me.' And Jesus says to him, 'Amen I say to you: Today, this very night, before the cock crows twice, you will deny me three times.' And he started to babble with great emphasis, 'Even if it is necessary for me to die with you, no way shall I deny you.' And they all talked in the same vein.

And they come to a place whose name is Gethsemani. And he says to his disciples, 'Sit here, while I pray.' And he takes along Peter and James and John with him. And he began to be distressed and in anxiety. And he says to them, 'My soul is very sad, even to death: remain here, and keep awake.' And going a little bit forward, he fell on the earth. And he prayed that if it were possible the hour might pass away from him. And he said, 'Abba, Father, everything is possible for you. Remove this cup from me.

But not "What do I want?" but "What do you want?".' And he comes and finds them sleeping, and he says to Peter, 'Simon, are you sleeping? Did you not have the strength to stay awake for a single hour? Watch and pray, that you may not come into temptation. The spirit is eager; but the flesh is sick.' And again he went off and prayed, saying the same thing. And again he came and found them sleeping. For their eyes were weighed down. And they didn't know what to say to him. And he comes the third time and says to them, 'Are you going to sleep and lounge about for the rest [of your lives]? That's it. The hour has come. Look! The Son of Man is being betrayed into the hands of sinners. Arise – let us go! Look: the one who betrays me has drawn near.'

Singing a hymn sounds cheerful enough; but there is not much else to be cheerful about, and the alert reader will in any case be reflecting that leaving the city for the Mountain of Olives sounds like a strategic withdrawal. Jesus warns them (citing the prediction of Zechariah 13:7) that they are on the point of abandoning him. All of them, but most especially Peter, protest the impossibility of this: 'even if all the others . . . even if it's necessary for me to die with you . . . '

Then he tells the disciples to sit, and takes the 'inner cabinet', and asks them simply to keep awake while he prays to the Father. Mark permits us to eavesdrop on his prayer: 'Abba Father' is the confident address; but the content is sad and fearful: 'Remove this cup from me.' Like all the best stories, this one comes in three parts, and each time, after his desperate prayer, Jesus finds the disciples asleep. That is all there is to it: we do not hear any response from the Father. Nevertheless it is noticeable that Jesus walks tall after this, so presumably something happened in the course of that prayer.

Have you found that prayer helps when circumstances are desperate?

The loneliness of Jesus

43-52 And immediately, while he was still speaking, Judas, one of the Twelve, appears, and with him a crowd with swords and cudgels, from the high priests and scribes and elders. The one who was betraying him had given them a secret signal, saying, 'The one whom I'll kiss – that's the one. Arrest him and lead him securely away.' And when he came he immediately came to him and says, 'Rabbi', and he kissed him. And they laid hands on him and arrested him. And one of the bystanders drawing his sword struck the High Priest's slave and took off his ear lobe. And Jesus responded and told them, 'As though I were a brigand, you've come out to seize me with swords and cudgels. Every day I was with you, teaching in the Temple: and you didn't arrest me. But let the scriptures be fulfilled.'

And they abandoned him; and every one of them fled.

And a certain young man was following along with him, wearing a linen cloth over his naked body. And they arrest him. But he cast aside the linen cloth and fled naked.

At this point, Jesus is arrested (by now that comes as no surprise); the arresting party is led, as Mark emphasises, by 'one of the Twelve', and comes, armed to the teeth, representing the religious authorities. The act of betrayal is performed with a formal greeting ('Rabbi'), and a kiss, which underlines the horror of it. A pathetic attempt at resistance (cutting off a slave's ear lobe!) is clearly both irrelevant and useless. Jesus is able to manage an ironic comment on what is happening; but no one else can manage anything at all: 'they abandoned him; and every one of them fled'. The mysterious young man who runs away naked could be absolutely anybody (scholars and other readers have made some interesting guesses!) – certainly one of his functions is to emphasise Jesus' utter loneliness.

The Sanhedrin looks for (and finds) evidence against Jesus

53-65 And they led Jesus to the High Priest, and all the high priests and elders and scribes came together. And Peter followed him from a long way off, right into the High Priest's courtyard. And he was sitting in with the other servants, and warming himself towards the light.

And the high priests and the whole Sanhedrin began to look for evidence against Jesus in order to put him to death. And they couldn't find [any]. For many gave false witness against him: and their evidence didn't match up. And some got up and bore false witness, to the effect: 'We heard him say, "I shall destroy this Temple made by hand, and in three days I shall build another, not made by hands."' And not even then did their evidence match up. And the High Priest rose up in the middle and interrogated Jesus, saying, 'Do you make no response? What evidence are these people bringing against you?' But he was silent, and made no response at all.

Again the High Priest interrogated him and says to him, 'Are you the Messiah, the son of the Blessed One?' And Jesus said, 'I AM. And "You will see the Son of Man sitting on the right side of power" and "coming with the clouds of heaven".' And the High Priest tore his garments and said, 'Why do we need any more witnesses? You heard the blasphemy. How does it seem to you?' And they all condemned him as liable to the death penalty. And some people began to spit on him and cover his head, and to strike him and say to him, 'Prophesy.' And the servants received him with blows.

Now comes the first judicial hearing, Jesus before the High Priest and Sanhedrin. Mark is quite clear that their aim is death, but also that they want some colourable evidence. There is a promising claim about destroying the Temple and building another in three days, which they might have linked with his prophetic gesture of driving out the commercial interests from the Temple, but since Jesus is saying nothing, there is not much going for them. Finally, the High Priest asks the question that has been lurking just below the surface of the text all the way through this Gospel: 'Are you the Messiah, the Son of the Blessed One?' We, the reader, have known the answer to this question since the Gospel's very first line, but it is nevertheless a surprise when Jesus roundly declares 'I AM' (quoting as he does so our old friends Daniel 7:13 and Psalm 110:1), and so allows the charge of blasphemy to have some substance.

Peter has never heard of Jesus

66-72 And Peter was still below in the courtyard. And there comes a single little slave girl of the High Priest. And seeing Peter warming himself she had a good look at him and says, 'You were also with the Nazarene, [that] Jesus.' And he denied it, saying, 'I neither know nor understand what you are saying.' And he went out into the forecourt. And the little slave girl saw him and began again to say to the bystanders, 'This [fellow] is from that lot.' And he again denied [it]. And again after a little the bystanders started to say to Peter, 'You must certainly be [one] of them: you're a Galilean.' And he began to curse and swear, 'I don't know this fellow you're talking about.'

And immediately for the second time a cock crowed. And Peter remembered the word, how Jesus had told him, 'Before the cock crows twice, three times you will deny me.'

And he thought of it and wept.

Jesus is not, it turns out, quite alone, because Peter has 'followed from a long way off'. Now, though, Peter is going to be tested (as Jesus had warned him). Absurdly (and Mark does nothing to hide the absurdity) the instrument of testing is the not very frightening figure of just one 'little slave girl', who says, quite correctly, 'You were with the Nazarene'. Peter won't admit that, under any circumstances, even when confronted with bystanders, and with the evidence of his dreadful Galilean accent: 'I don't know the fellow you're talking about.' Then the cock crows, and Peter remembers, and dissolves into saving and healing tears.

Is not this one of the saddest tales you have ever heard?

Pilate reluctantly agrees to Jesus' death

15 1-15 And immediately, early in the morning, they held a consultation, the high priests with the elders and scribes and the whole Sanhedrin. And they bound Jesus and led him away and handed him over to Pilate. And Pilate interrogated him, 'You are the "King of the Jews"?' But he answered and said, 'You say so.' And the high priests made many accusations against him. And Pilate interrogated him again, saying, 'You do not respond? Look how many things they accuse you of!' But Jesus no longer made any response, so that Pilate wondered.

Now at the feast he used to free for them one prisoner whom they requested. And there was the one known as Barabbas, who had been imprisoned with the revolutionaries who had committed murder in the revolt. And the crowd came up and began to ask [Pilate to do] what he used to do for them. And Pilate responded to them, saying, 'Do you want me to release the "King of the Jews" to you?' For he knew that it was out of spite that the high priests had handed him over. And the high priests incited the crowd that he should rather release Barabbas to them. And Pilate again responded; and he was saying to them, 'So what do you want me to do with the "King of the Jews"?' And they again screamed out, 'Crucify him.' And Pilate tried to say to them, 'Why? What crime has he committed?' And they screamed out all the more, 'Crucify him.'

Then Pilate, wanting to do enough [to please] the crowd, released Barabbas to them. And he handed Jesus over to be crucified, having scourged him.

The Sanhedrin now holds a second session, after which they finally bring the local Roman governor into the matter. Pilate hardly knows what is going on, despairingly asking if Jesus is 'King of the Jews' (about the only concept he can grasp); like the High Priest before him, he gets nothing out of Jesus. Nor, when he tries to release Jesus, does he get anything out of the crowd (which Mark blames on the high priests). Everyone seems, on this account, agreed that Jesus has done nothing to deserve it; but there he is, being scourged in preparation for a horrible death.

Whose side are you on?

The journey to Golgotha

16-24 And the soldiers led him inside the courtyard, which is the praetorium. And they call together the whole cohort. And they clothe him in purple and place on him a thorny wreath which they wove. And they began to acclaim him, 'Hail, King of the Jews.' And they started to beat his head with a reed; and they were spitting on him, and they were kneeling down and worshipping him.

And when they had mocked him, they took the purple off him, and put his own clothes on him. And they take him out to crucify him.

And they conscript a certain passer-by, Simon, a Cyrenean coming in from the countryside, the father of Alexander and Rufus, to carry his cross. And they take him to the place Golgotha, which when it is translated is 'Place of the Skull'. And they tried to give him wine flavoured with myrrh – but he didn't take it. And they crucify him. And they 'divide his garments, casting a lot over them [to see] who would get something'.

Two quite different things happen now. First, the soldiers, picking up the idea that 'this one thinks he's a king!' have a little game, dressing him up and doing a horrible parody of respect for a king. Second, though, these same soldiers conscript an African to help Jesus. Mark tells us that this Simon is 'the father of Alexander and Rufus'; now the only reason Mark mentions their names must be that his church knows them. So something must have happened to Simon of Cyrene that day, to turn his sons into disciples; and that is the first bit of good news that we have had for a long time. Someone tries to reduce Jesus' pain by giving him 'wine flavoured with myrrh', but he refuses, and Golgotha lives up to its grim name, as they squabble over who's to have his clothes.

The quotation about 'dividing his garments' is from Psalm 22:18. The early Christians had clearly meditated on this psalm, to try and find some meaning in the awful event of Jesus' crucifixion. Jesus' dying words, in the next section, may well be a quotation of its opening line. Read through the psalm, and see what other details surface in Mark's text hereabouts.

What do you think happened to Simon of Cyrene that day?

A very lonely death

25-37 Now it was the third hour, and they crucified him. And the inscription of his charge was inscribed 'The King of the Jews'. And with him they crucify two brigands, one on [the] right and one on his left. And the passers-by started to blaspheme him, nodding their heads and saying, 'Aha! The chap who destroys the Temple and builds it in three days! Save yourself [by] coming down from the cross!' Likewise the high priests were making mocking comments to each other, along with the scribes, 'He saved others; himself he cannot save. Let the "Messiah", the "King of Israel", come down from the cross, now, so that we may see and believe.'

Even those crucified along with him reviled him.

And when it came to the sixth hour, darkness came on the whole land until the ninth hour. And at the ninth hour Jesus shouted in a loud voice, 'Eloi, eloi, lema sabachthani?' which when it is translated is, 'My God, my God, for what purpose did you abandon me?' And some of the bystanders, hearing [this], started to say, 'Look – he is calling on Elijah.' And someone ran and filled a sponge with vinegar and put it round a stick and gave it to him to drink, saying, 'Wait – let's see if Elijah is coming to take him down. But Jesus, letting out a great shout, expired.

Now Mark, with unusual exactness, tells us that Jesus was on the cross for six agonising hours. On his right and left, in a terrible parody of a ruler's enthronement, are his two 'co-rulers', whom Mark dismisses as 'brigands'. Then, instead of the normal fawning sycophancy, Jesus gets abuse from passers-by, 'Save yourself'; from high priests and scribes, 'Let the "Messiah", the "King of Israel", come down from the cross now'; and finally from his fellow-convicts.

Then comes Nature's comment on what is happening: 'darkness . . . until the ninth hour', and a heart-rending cry of loneliness: 'My God, my God, for what purpose did you abandon me?' Some readers note that these are the opening words of Psalm 22, which ends with an encouraging cry of joy. That may be so, but Mark quotes the phrase in Jesus' native Aramaic, not in the Hebrew in which the Psalms were written, and I think that Mark intends us to feel the loneliness. No one understands him, anyway – they think that perhaps Elijah may drop in. As we hear this, we reflect that hope was not very far below the surface of those who watched Jesus die: perhaps after all, he might have been the real thing . . . ?

Was *Jesus the 'real thing'?*

The final, remarkable verdict

38, 39 And the veil of the Temple was torn in two, from the top to the very bottom. And seeing that he expired in this way, the centurion who stood by, over against him, said, 'Truly this man was Son of God.'

Now that Jesus is safely dead, we hear the verdict on his life. First there is the tearing of the Temple veil. Clearly we are intended to read this as

God's comment on Jesus' death, and on the part played in it by the Temple authorities.

The second verdict is even more remarkable. For the centurion who has watched Jesus die in this appalling, and appallingly lonely, way now gives his comment: 'Truly this man was Son of God.' Now we, the reader, have known this since the opening line of the Gospel, and even if we hadn't, we have twice heard God saying so. This verdict, on the lips of such a man, is the climax of the Gospel's remarkable treatment of who Jesus is: a mysterious and very different Messiah, but Messiah and Son of God nevertheless.

The circumstances of Jesus' burial

40-47 And there were women looking at him from afar, among whom were also Mary the Magdalene, and Mary mother of James the Little and of Joses, and Salome, the women who when he was in the Galilee used to follow him and minister to him, and many other women who came with him up to Jerusalem.

And when it had already become late, since it was Preparation Day, which is the day before the Sabbath, there came Joseph, the one from Arimathea. He was a reputable councillor; and he was also waiting for the kingdom of God. He was daring enough to go to Pilate and ask for the body of Jesus. And Pilate wondered if he was already dead [or: was surprised that he should be already dead]. And he summoned the centurion and asked if he was long dead. And when he had confirmation from the centurion, he gifted the corpse to Joseph. And he bought a linen cloth and took him down and wrapped him in the linen cloth and placed him in a tomb which was hewn out of rock. And he rolled a stone on to the door of the tomb.

And Mary the Magdalene and Mary [the mother] of Joses were watching where he lay.

Jesus was properly dead, no question about it, and now we see him buried. First, though, we discover that he was not as alone as we had feared: it turns out that the brave women were there, who had followed him from Galilee. Then a male follower of Jesus comes out of the woodwork: Joseph of Arimathea, whom we have not heard of before, but who is clearly quite serious about his discipleship. Finally (in case we should wonder if anyone actually knew where the tomb was), we learn that two women were at the site.

Three endings to the Gospel

16 1-20 And when the Sabbath was at last over, Mary the Magdalene, and Mary of James, and Salome bought spices in order to come and anoint him. And extremely early on the first of the Sabbaths they come to the tomb. The sun had already risen. And they said to themselves, 'Who will roll away the stone for us from the door of the tomb?' And looking up [or: recovering their sight] they see that the stone has been rolled away. For it was very big. And going into the tomb they saw a young man sitting on the right wearing a white robe. And they were alarmed. But he

said to the women, 'Do not be alarmed. You seek Jesus the Nazarene, the one who was crucified. He is risen; he is not here. See the place where they put him. But go, tell his disciples, and Peter, that "he is going before you [or: leading you] into the Galilee. There you will see him, as he said to you".' And going out they fled from the tomb, for quivering and astonishment had hold of them. And they said nothing to anybody. For they were afraid . . .

Most scholars today regard this as the original ending of Mark's Gospel, and the 'long' and short endings, printed overleaf, as additions made by people who were not the original author, and who regarded this as an unsuitable ending. But it is a marvellous passage: you can feel the impatience of these women, as they grind their way through the Sabbath, before they can buy spices to do the needful for Jesus' dead body (and notice, by the way, that they evidently did not believe in the Resurrection; you can only anoint dead bodies if they stay where they are put). Mark makes, perhaps, a little joke at their expense, when he says that 'the sun had already risen'; and if the reader is inclined to berate the women for their improvidence in not thinking in advance about how to roll the stone away, then just ask where Jesus' male followers are at this moment. Then there is the young man, and the information that he already has, and the precious proclamation that he gives them: 'he is risen'. Then there is the flight of the women; but there is a clue even there: 'quivering and astonishment' is a sign of the presence of God. This is a powerful ending.

Who do you think the 'young man' is?

Do you really think that the women said 'nothing to anybody'? What is Mark saying to us here?

The 'long ending' [16:9-20]	The 'short ending'
But being resurrected early on the first day of the week he appeared to Mary the Magdalene, from whom he had cast out seven demons. She went and announced to those with him, who had taken to mourning and weeping. And they, hearing that he was alive and had been seen by her did not believe [or: had no faith]. And after this he appeared in a different form to two of them who were walking to the country. And they went and announced it to the rest. And they did not even believe *them*. Later, he appeared to the eleven themselves as they were at table and he reproached them for their faithlessness and hardness of heart, because they had not believed those who had seen him resurrected. And he said to them, 'Go into the whole world. Proclaim the gospel to all creation. The one who believes and is baptised will be saved; but the faithless [or: the one who does not believe] will be condemned. These signs will follow those who do believe: in my name, they will expel demons. They will speak in new languages. And in their hands they will lift up snakes. And if they drink anything lethal it will not harm them. They will lay hands on the sick and they will be well.' And so the Lord Jesus after speaking to them was taken up into heaven and sat at the right hand of God. Meanwhile they went out and preached everywhere, the Lord working with them and confirming their word through the signs that followed them.	They concisely proclaimed all the instructions to those [who were gathered] around Peter. And after this, Jesus himself, from east as far as the west sent out through them the holy and imperishable proclamation of eternal salvation. Amen.

In a fit of generosity, the manuscripts now give us not one but three endings to the Gospel. The 'long ending' and the 'short ending' probably suggest an attempt by later authors to patch up what they thought to be Mark's failure to produce a proper ending. The 'long ending' is really a series of scenes taken from other Gospels and from Acts, while the 'short ending' is just a way of bringing the story to a suitable conclusion.

It looks, therefore, as though the Gospel originally ended at 16:8, 'And they said nothing to anybody. For they were afraid . . . ' Now it may have been rats or mice that ate the original ending of the manuscript. But as we have read the Gospel together, we have seen how mysterious it is, with its subtle portrayal of what Jesus is like, and what his disciples must be like; and certainly such an ending would fit. And, of course, we know that the women must have said something to someone, or we should not be reading this extraordinary Gospel.

What is Jesus like? What must his disciples be like?

Palestine of the New Testament
Herod's Fortress
Tyre
SYRO-PHOENICIA
Caesarea Philippi (Paneas)
Trachonitis
Lake Huleh
Batanea
Gaulanitis
Cadas
Gischala
GALILEE
Ptolemais (Akko)
Chorazin
Bethsaida-Julias
Capernaum
Gennesaret
Dion
Magdala
Sea of Galilee
Gergesa
Mt Carmel
Tiberias
Abila
Asochis
Cana
Sepphoris
Nazareth
R. Yarmuk
Mt Tabor
Dora
Plain of Esdraelon
Nain
Crocodilon
THE GREAT SEA
Caesarea Maritima
DECAPOLIS
Pella
SAMARIA
Aenon
R. Jordan
Plain of Sharon
Sebaste (Samaria)
Gerasa
Mt Ebal
Sychar
Mt Gerizim
R. Jabbok
PERAEA
Antipatris
Jaffa
Gadara
Arimathaea
Philadelphia
Lydda
Ephraim
Jamnia
Jericho
Emmaus
Betharamphtha
Jerusalem
Ein-Kerem
Bethpage
Azotus
Bethany
Qumran
JUDAEA
Bethlehem
Ashkelon
Marisa
Bethsura
Gaza
Hebron
Dead Sea
En-gedi
R. Arnon
NABATAEAN KINGDOM
IDUMAEA
Masada

NOTES